Best Garden Plants *for* Alberta

Donna Dawson *Laura Peters*

LONE PINE PUBLISHING

The Publisher: Lone Pine Publishing

10145 – 81 Avenue

Edmonton, AB T6E 1W9 Canada

Website: www.lonepinepublishing.com

1808 B Street NW, Suite 140

Auburn, WA, USA 98001

Library and Archives Canada Cataloguing in Publication

Dawson, Donna, 1951-
Best garden plants for Alberta / Donna Dawson, Laura Peters.

Includes index.
ISBN-13: 978-1-55105-479-7
ISBN-10: 1-55105-479-5

Plants, Ornamental—Alberta. 2. Gardening—Alberta.
I. Peters, Laura, 1968- II. Title.
SB453.3.C2D39 2005   635.9'097123   C2004-905744-8

Editorial Director: Nancy Foulds
Project Editors & Editorial: Gary Whyte, Rachelle Delaney
Photo Editor: Don Williamson
Production Manager: Gene Longson
Book Design & Layout: Heather Markham
Cover Design: Gerry Dotto
Image Editing: Trina Koscielnuk, Elliot Engley
Scanning & Electronic Film: Elite Lithographers Co.

Photography: All photos by Tim Matheson, Tamara Eder or Laura Peters except AAFC 70a, 131b; AA Selection 35a; Agriculture Canada 127a&b; J.C. Bakker & Sons 128a; Brendan Casement 86a&b, 106a; Janet Davis 131a; Dean Didur 80a; Don Doucette 90a, 113b; EuroAmerican 13a; Jen Fafard 145a; Derek Fell 11a, 46b; Erika Flatt 94a, 143a, 146a, 167b, 169a&b; Anne Gordon 139b, 140b; Horticolor 134b; Linda Kershaw 78b; Liz Klose 121a, 149a, 151a, 152a&b, 160a, 163a, 164a, 166a, 170a&b; Dawn Loewen 66a, 76a, 78a, 81a, 85a&b; Janet Loughrey 32a, 139a; Marilynn McAra 145b; Steve Nikkila 104a; Kim O'Leary 72a, 155b; Allison Penko 76b, 93b, 101a, 105a, 109a&b, 112b, 165a, 166b; Robert Ritchie 99a, 111b, 124a&b, 125a&b, 126a&b, 129a, 130a&b, 135a, 137a; Leila Sidi 148b; Joy Spurr 134a; Peter Thompstone 30a, 53a, 61a&b, 65a; Mark Turner 72b; Don Williamson 137b, 143b, 144a&b, 148a; Tim Wood 113a, 114b.

This book is not intended as a "how-to" guide for eating garden plants. No plant or plant extract should be consumed unless you are certain of its identity and toxicity and of your potential for allergic reactions.

We acknowledge the financial support of the Government of Canada through the Book Publishing Industry Development Program (BPIDP) for our publishing activities.

PC: P1

Table of Contents

We would like to thank the following for their valuable time and beautiful images: Peter Thompstone, Euro American, U of A Devonian Botanical Gardens, Muttart Conservatory, Proven Winners, Don Doucette, AAFC Morden, AA Selections, US National Arboretum, Brendan Casement, Bruce Dancik and everyone who allowed us to photograph their gardens.

Introduction

Starting a garden can seem like a daunting task. Which plants should you choose? Where should you put them in the garden? This book is intended to give beginning gardeners the information they need to start planning and planting gardens of their own. It describes a wide variety of plants and provides basic planting information such as where and how to plant.

Lying on the lee side of the mountains, Alberta escapes British Columbia's coastal downpours and is blessed with more sunny days than any other Canadian province. Cold winters and temperate summers are normal, but Alberta's winters are generally less cold than those of Saskatchewan or Manitoba. Edmonton, the northernmost of Canada's provincial capitals, averages about 15° C (60°F) in summer but only a brisk –13° C (9°F) in January, while Calgary boasts similar summer temperatures but an average of –9° C (16°F) early in the new year.

The southwestern portion of the province experiences a unique winter phenomenon called the Chinook. These can rapidly warm Alberta temperatures by as much as 20° C (36°F) in a matter of hours. Chinooks occur when dry air from the Pacific Ocean is heated as it flows down the slopes of the Rockies.

Precipitation is relatively consistent throughout the province. However, owing to Chinooks, the southernmost snow cover disappears much more quickly than snow in the north.

Hardiness zones and frost dates are two terms often used when discussing climate. Hardiness zones consider the temperatures and conditions in winter. Plants are rated based on the zones in which they grow successfully. The last frost date in spring and the first frost date in fall allow us to predict the length of the growing season. Winter protection and a sheltered location may be necessary for plants grown outside their hardiness zones.

Getting Started

When planning your garden, start with a quick analysis of the garden as it is now. Plants have different requirements and it is best to put the right plant in the right place rather than try to change your garden to suit the plants you want.

Knowing which parts of your garden receive the most and least amounts of sunlight will help you choose the proper plants and decide where to plant them. Light is classified into four basic groups: full sun (direct, unobstructed light all or most of the day); partial shade (direct sun for about half the day and shade for the rest); light shade (shade all or most of the day with some sun filtering through to ground level); and full shade (no direct sunlight). Most plants prefer a certain amount of light, but many can adapt to a range of light levels.

Plants use the soil to hold themselves upright, but also rely on the many resources it holds: air, water, nutrients, organic matter and a host of microbes. The particle size of the soil influences the amount of air, water and nutrients it can hold. Sand, with the largest particles, has lots of air space and allows water and nutrients to drain quickly. Clay, with the smallest particles, is high in nutrients but has very little air space. Water is therefore slow to penetrate clay and slow to drain from it.

Soil acidity or alkalinity (measured on the pH scale) influences the nutrients available to plants. A pH of 7 is neutral; a lower pH is more acidic. Most plants prefer a soil with a pH of 5.5–7.5. Soil-testing kits are available at most garden centres, and soil samples can be sent to testing facilities for a more thorough analysis.

Japanese spurge is an out-of-zone plant.

Compost is one of the best and most important amendments you can add to any type of soil. Compost improves soil by adding organic matter and nutrients, introducing soil microbes, increasing water retention and improving drainage. Compost can be purchased or you can make it in your own backyard.

Average Annual Minimum Temperature

0a	0b
1a	1b
2a	2b
3a	3b
4a	

Microclimates are small areas that are generally warmer or colder than the surrounding area. Buildings, fences, trees and other large structures can provide extra shelter in winter, but may trap heat in summer, thus creating a warmer microclimate. The bottoms of hills are usually colder than the tops, but may not be as windy. Take advantage of these areas when you plan your garden and choose your plants; you may even grow out-of-zone plants successfully in a warm, sheltered location.

Selecting Plants

It's important to purchase healthy plants that are free of pests and diseases. Such plants will establish quickly in your garden and won't introduce problems that may spread to other plants. You should have a good idea of what the plant is supposed to look like—the colour and shape of the leaves and the habit of the plant—and then inspect the plant for signs of disease or infestation.

The majority of plants are container grown. This is an efficient way for nurseries and greenhouses to grow plants, but when plants grow in a restricted space for too long, they can become pot bound with their roots densely encircling the inside of the pot. Avoid purchasing plants in this condition; they are often stressed and can take longer to establish. In some cases they may not establish at all. It is often possible to remove pots temporarily to look at the condition of the roots. You can check for soil-borne insects and rotten roots at the same time.

Planting Basics

The following tips apply to all plants.

• Prepare the garden before planting. Dig over the soil, pull up any weeds and make any needed amendments before you begin planting, if possible. This may be more difficult in established beds to which you want to add a single plant. The prepared area should be at least twice the size of the plant you want to put in, and preferably the expected size of the mature plant.

• Settle the soil with water. Good contact between the roots and the soil is important, but if you press the soil down too firmly, as often happens when you step on the soil, you can cause compaction, which reduces the movement of water through the soil and leaves very few air spaces. Instead, pour water in as you fill the hole with soil. The water will settle the soil evenly without allowing it to compact.

• Unwrap the roots. It is always best to remove any container before planting to give roots the chance to spread out naturally when planted. In particular, you should remove plastic containers, fibre pots, wire and burlap before planting trees. Fibre pots decompose very slowly, if at all, and wick moisture away from the plant. Burlap may be synthetic, and won't decompose, and wire can strangle the roots as they mature. The only exceptions to this

1. Gently remove container.

2. Ensure proper planting depth.

3. Backfill with amended soil.

rule are peat pots and pellets used to start annuals and vegetables; these decompose and can be planted with the young transplants.

• Accommodate the rootball. If you prepared your planting spot ahead of time, your planting hole will only need to be big enough to accommodate the root ball with the roots spread out slightly.

• Know the mature size. Plant based on how big plants will grow rather than how big they are when you plant them. Large plants should have enough room to mature without interfering with walls, roof overhangs, power lines and walkways.

• Plant at the same depth. Plants like to grow at a certain level in relation to the soil and should be planted at the same level they were before you transplanted them.

• Identify your plants. Keep track of what's what in your garden by putting a tag next to your plant when you plant it. It is very easy for beginning gardeners to forget exactly what they planted and where they planted it. I always tag new transplants and each spring I get a surprise. Either something comes back that I forgot I planted, or I can't for the life of me identify the dead brown stubs that evidently did not survive the winter.

• Water deeply and infrequently. It's better to water deeply once every week or two rather than water a little bit more often. This forces roots to grow as they search for water and helps them survive dry spells when water bans may restrict your watering

Annuals & perennials in a mixed border

regime. Always check the root zone before you water. More gardeners overwater than underwater.

Annuals

Annuals are planted new each year and are only expected to last for a single growing season. Their flowers and decorative foliage provide bright splashes of colour and can fill in spaces around immature trees, shrubs and perennials.

Annuals are easy to plant and are usually sold in small packs of four or six. The roots quickly fill the space in these small packs, so the small rootball should be broken up before planting. I often break

4. Settle backfilled soil with water.

5. Water the plant well.

6. Add a layer of mulch.

Trees & shrubs provide colour and interest year-round.

Trees & Shrubs

Trees and shrubs provide the bones of the garden. They are often the slowest growing plants, but usually live the longest. Characterized by leaf type, they may be deciduous or evergreen, and needled or broad-leaved.

Trees should have as little disturbed soil as possible at the bottom of the planting hole. Loose dirt settles over time and sinking even an inch can kill some trees.

Staking, sometimes recommended for newly planted trees, is only necessary for trees over 1.5 m (5') tall.

Pruning is more often required for shrubs than trees. It helps them maintain an attractive shape and can improve blooming. Consult a book on pruning or take a pruning course for information about pruning trees and shrubs.

Roses

Roses are beautiful shrubs with lovely, often fragrant blooms. Traditionally, most roses only bloomed once in the growing season, but currently available varieties

the ball in two up the centre or run my thumb up each side to break up the roots.

Many annuals are grown from seed and can be started directly in the garden.

Perennials

Perennials grow for three or more years. They usually die back to the ground each fall and send up new shoots in spring, though some are evergreen. They often have a shorter period of bloom than annuals, but require less care.

Many perennials benefit from being divided every few years. This keeps them growing and blooming vigorously, and in some cases controls their spread. Dividing involves digging the plant up, removing dead bits, breaking the plant into several pieces and replanting some or all of the pieces. Extra pieces can be given as gifts to family, friends and neighbours. Consult a perennial book such as *Perennials for Alberta* for further information on the care of perennials.

Roses are lovely on their own or in mixed borders.

often bloom more than once during the warm summer months.

Generally, roses prefer a fertile, well-prepared planting area. A rule of thumb is to prepare an area 60 cm (24") across, front to back and side to side, and 60 cm (24") deep. Add plenty of compost or other fertile organic matter and keep roses well watered during the growing season. Many roses are quite durable and will adapt to poorer conditions.

Roses, like all shrubs, have specific pruning requirements. Consult a reputable rose book for detailed information.

Vines

Vines or climbing plants are useful for screening and shade, especially in a location too small for a tree. They may be woody or herbaceous and annual or perennial.

Most vines need supports, and often, sturdy supports upon which to grow. Trellises, arbours, porch railings, fences, walls, poles and trees are all possible supports. If a support is needed, ensure it's in place before you plant the vine to avoid disturbing the roots later.

Virginia creeper provides a shot of red in autumn.

Bulbs

The bulb section of this book includes some plants that grow from corms, tubers and rhizomes. All of these plants have fleshy underground storage organs that allow them to survive extended periods of dormancy. They are often grown for the bright splashes of colour their flowers provide. They may be spring, summer or fall flowering.

Hardy bulbs can be left in the ground and will flower every year, but many popular tender plants grow from bulbs, corms or tubers. These tender plants are generally lifted from the garden in fall as the foliage dies back, and are stored in a cool, frost-free location for winter, to be replanted in spring.

Calla rhizomes need to be lifted before winter.

Herbs

Herbs may be medicinal or culinary and often both. A few common culinary herbs are listed in this book. Even if you don't cook with them, the often-fragrant foliage adds its aroma to the garden and the plants can be quite decorative in form, leaf and flower.

Many herbs have pollen-producing flowers that attract butterflies, bees and hummingbirds to your garden. They also attract predatory insects. These useful

Grow herbs in containers close to the kitchen door.

Ornamental grasses are becoming very popular additions to the garden. Grasses offer a variety of textures and foliage colors, and at least three seasons of interest. There is an ornamental grass for every garden situation and condition. Some grasses thrive in any garden condition, from hot and dry to cool and wet, and in all types of soils. Ornamental grasses have very few insect or disease problems. They require little maintenance other than cutting the perennial grasses back in fall or spring.

Ferns are ancient plants that have adapted to many different environments. The fern family is a very large group of plants with interesting foliage in a wide array of shapes and colors. Ferns do not produce flowers, but instead reproduce by spores borne in interesting structures on the undersides and margins of the foliage. Ferns are generally planted in moist, shaded gardens, but some will thrive in dry shade under dense evergreens, such as spruce and pine.

insects help to manage your pest problems by feasting on problem insects such as aphids, mealy bugs and whiteflies.

Ornamental Grasses, Foliar Plants & Ferns

Foliage is an important consideration for your garden. Although many plants look spectacular in bloom, they can seem dull without flowers. Including a variety of plants with unique, interesting, or striking foliage in your garden can provide all the color and texture you want without the need to rely on flowers.

We have included some grass-like foliage plants in this book. Rush has grass-like foliage and can be used with or as a substitute for ornamental grasses. We have also added a variety of plants grown for their foliage throughout the book. Many annuals, perennials, trees, shrubs, vines and herbs have wonderful foliage, and will be an asset to your garden landscape.

A Final Comment

Don't be afraid to experiment. No matter how many books you read, trying things yourself is the best way to learn and to find out what will grow in your garden. Use the information provided as guidelines, and have fun!

Many ornamental grasses are well suited to Alberta's climate.

African Daisy
Osteospermum

African daisies are colourful, care-free plants that retain their good looks late into fall and can withstand temperatures as low as –4° C (25° F). New varieties have better heat and moisture tolerance.

Growing

Plant in **full sun** in **light, evenly moist, moderately fertile, well-drained** soil when the soil warms in spring. Do not overwater or let the plants wilt; use organic mulch to cut down on watering. Deadhead to encourage new growth and more flowers. Pinch young plants to encourage a bushier form.

Tips

African daisies work well in containers or beds. Their flowers look great mixed with plants like petunias or verbenas.

Recommended

O. ecklonis grows upright to almost prostrate, but it is often rejected in favour of its wonderful cultivars. **Passion Mix** has free-flowering, heat-tolerant plants. The **Springstar Series** boasts compact, early-flowering plants. **Starwhirls Series** flowers have unique spoon-shaped petals.

Proven Winners' **O. Symphony Series** has mounding plants. They tolerate heat well and flower through the summer.

You may find African daisy listed as either Dimorphotheca *or* Osteospermum. Dimorphotheca *is a closely related genus that formerly included all the plants now listed as* Osteospermum.

Also called: Cape daisy **Features:** colourful flowers, easy care, heat tolerance **Flower colour:** white, peach, orange, yellow, pink, lavender, purple; often with dark centres of blue-purple or other colours **Height:** 30–50 cm (12–20") **Spread:** 25–50 cm (10–20")

Angelonia
Angelonia

*W*ith its loose, airy spikes of orchid-like flowers, Angelonia makes a welcome addition to the garden.

The individual flowers look a bit like orchid blossoms, but angelonia is actually from the same family as snapdragon.

Growing

Angelonia prefers **full sun** but tolerates a bit of shade. The soil should be **fertile, moist** and **well drained**. Although this plant grows naturally in damp areas, such as along ditches and near ponds, it is fairly drought tolerant. Plant out after the chance of frost has passed.

Tips

Angelonia makes a good addition to an annual or mixed border and looks most attractive when planted in groups. It is also suited to a pondside or streamside planting.

Recommended

A. angustifolia is a bushy, upright plant with loose spikes of flowers in varied shades of purple. Cultivars with white or bicoloured flowers are available.

Also called: angel wings, summer snapdragon
Features: attractive flowers **Flower colour:** purple, blue, white **Height:** 30–60 cm (12–24")
Spread: 30 cm (12")

Bacopa
Sutera

Bacopa snuggles under and around the stems of taller plants, forming a dense carpet dotted with tiny, white to pale lavender flowers, and eventually drifting over pot edges to form a waterfall of stars.

Growing

Bacopa grows well in **partial shade**, with protection from the hot afternoon sun. The soil should be of **average fertility**, **humus rich**, **moist** and **well drained**.

Don't allow this plant to dry out, or the leaves will quickly die. Cutting back dead growth may encourage new shoots.

Tips

Bacopa is a popular plant for hanging baskets, mixed containers and window boxes. It is not recommended as a bedding plant because it fizzles quickly when the weather gets hot, particularly if you forget to water. Plant it where you will see it every day so you will remember to water it.

Recommended

S. cordata is a compact, trailing plant that bears small, white flowers all summer. Cultivars with larger white flowers, lavender flowers or gold and green variegated foliage are available.

Bacopa is a perennial that is grown as an annual outdoors. It will thrive as a houseplant in a bright room.

Features: decorative flowers, foliage and habit **Flower colour:** white, lavender **Height:** 8–15 cm (3–6") **Spread:** 30–50 cm (12–20")

Begonia
Begonia

With its beautiful flowers, compact habit and decorative foliage, a begonia—any of the many varieties—is sure to fulfill your shade gardening needs.

Growing

Light or **partial shade** is best, though some wax begonias tolerate sun if their soil is kept moist. The soil should be **fertile, rich in organic matter** and **well drained** with a **neutral** or **acidic pH**. Allow the soil to dry out slightly between waterings, particularly for tuberous begonias. Begonias love warm weather—plant them after the soil warms in spring. If they sit in cold soil, they may become stunted and fail to thrive.

Tips

All begonias are useful for shaded garden beds and planters. The trailing tuberous varieties can be used in hanging baskets and along rock walls where the flowers will cascade over the edges. Wax begonias, with their neat, rounded habits, are attractive as edging plants. Rex begonias, with their dramatic foliage, are useful as specimen plants in containers and beds.

Recommended

B. **Rex Cultorum Hybrids** (rex begonias) are grown for their dramatic, colourful foliage.

B. semperflorens (wax begonias) have pink, white, red or bicoloured flowers and green, bronze, reddish or white-variegated foliage.

B. x *tuberhybrida* (tuberous begonias) are generally sold as tubers and are popular for their flowers in many shades of red, pink, yellow, orange or white.

Wax begonias are generally pest free and bloom all summer, even without deadheading.

Features: colourful flowers, decorative foliage
Flower colour: pink, white, red, yellow, orange, bicoloured or picotee **Height:** 15–60 cm (6–24") **Spread:** 15–60 cm (6–24")

Calendula

Calendula

Calendulas are bright and charming. They produce attractive flowers in warm colours all summer and fall.

Growing

Calendula does equally well in **full sun** or **partial shade**. It likes cool weather and can withstand a moderate frost. The soil should be of **average fertility** and **well drained**. Deadhead to prolong blooming and keep plants looking neat. If plants fade in summer heat, cut them back to 10–15 cm (4–6") above the ground to promote new growth, or pull them up and seed new ones. Either method will provide a good fall display. Sow seed directly into the garden in mid-spring.

Tips

This informal plant looks attractive in borders, mixed into the vegetable patch, and in mixed planters. Calendula is a cold-hardy annual and often continues flowering, even through a layer of snow, until the ground freezes completely.

Recommended

C. officinalis is a vigorous, tough, upright plant that bears daisy-like, single or double flowers in a wide range of yellow and orange shades. Several cultivars are available.

Calendula flowers are popular kitchen herbs that can be added to stews for colour or salads for flavouring. They can also be brewed into an infusion that is useful as a wash for minor cuts and bruises.

Also called: pot marigold, English marigold
Features: colourful flowers, long blooming period **Flower colour:** cream, yellow, gold, orange, apricot **Height:** 25–60 cm (10–24")
Spread: 20–50 cm (8–20")

Cape Daisy
Arctotis (Venidium)

This is no ordinary daisy. The large, showy flowers stand tall above the coarse but full foliage and demand your attention. It comes as no surprise that this plant is native to parts of Africa, because its heat and drought tolerance are second to none.

Growing

Cape daisy will thrive in **full sun**. **Sharply drained, moist, light** soil is best. Cut the flower stems back to the spent crown to encourage further blooming.

Tips

This unusual annual looks like a cross between a gazania and a daisy. The foliage looks rugged and coarse. Cape daisies suit mixed borders when planted in large groups for impact. This annual is incredibly drought tolerant and thrives in containers placed in full sun.

Recommended

A. fastuosa (*V. fastuosum*) produces deeply lobed, silvery white, fuzzy leaves. Tall flower stalks produce deep orange daisy-like flowers with large black-brown centres surrounded by dark rings. 'Zulu Prince' is a new cultivar that offers intense, silvery white foliage covered in dense, woolly hairs. The flowers are quite large, with dark centres surrounded by creamy white petals banded with purple-brown and orange rings at the base of each petal.

The cultivars produce flowers that tend to stay open longer than the species. The flowers are known to close in the afternoon and on overcast days.

Also called: African daisy, monarch of the veldt **Features:** large, daisy-like flowers; fuzzy silver foliage; growth habit **Flower colour:** yellow, orange, white **Height:** 30–60 cm (12–24") **Spread:** 30 cm (12")

Coleus

Solenostemon (Coleus)

From brash yellows, oranges and reds to deep maroon and rose selections, coleus colours, textures and variations are almost limitless.

Growing

Coleus prefers to grow in **light** or **partial shade,** but tolerates full shade that isn't too dense and full sun if the plants are watered regularly. The soil should be of **rich to average fertility, humus rich, moist** and **well drained.**

Place the seeds in a refrigerator for one or two days before planting them on the soil surface; the cold temperatures will help break the seeds' dormancy. They need light to germinate. Seedlings are green at first, but leaf variegation will develop as the plants mature.

Tips

The bold, colourful foliage looks dramatic when coleus are grouped as edging plants or in beds, borders or mixed containers. Coleus can also be grown indoors as a houseplant in a bright room.

Pinch off flower buds when they develop; the plants tend to stretch out and become less attractive after they flower.

Recommended

S. scutellarioides (*Coleus blumei* var. *verschaffeltii*) forms a bushy mound of foliage. The leaf edges range from slightly toothed to very ruffled. Leaves are usually multi-coloured, with shades ranging from pale greenish yellow to deep purple-black. Many of the dozens of cultivars cannot be started from seed.

Coleus can be trained to grow into a standard (tree) form; simply pinch off the side branches as they grow. Once the plant reaches the desired height, pinch from the top.

Features: brightly coloured foliage
Flower colour: light purple, grown as a foliage plant **Height:** 15–90 cm (6–36")
Spread: usually equal to height

Cosmos
Cosmos

Cosmos flowers are deeply saturated with colour and provide nectar for various butterflies. Their fluted petals add an interesting texture to the garden and the flower vase.

Growing
Cosmos like **full sun**. The soil should be of **poor** or **average fertility** and **well drained**. Cosmos are drought tolerant. Overfertilizing and overwatering can reduce the number of flowers produced. Keep faded blooms cut to encourage more buds. Often, these plants reseed themselves.

Tips
Cosmos look attractive planted in cottage gardens, at the back of a border or en masse in an informal bed or border. Taller varieties will likely need staking.

Recommended
Look for *C. atrosanguineus* (chocolate cosmos); on a hot day it smells like chocolate.

C. bipinnatus (annual cosmos) has many cultivars. The flowers come in a variety of colours, usually with yellow centres. Old varieties grow tall, while some of the newer cultivars remain quite short. **Sea Shells Series** has flowers in all colours and petals that are rolled into tubes.

When cut, cosmos flowers make lovely, long-lasting fillers in arrangements.

Features: colourful flowers and fern-like foliage
Flower colour: white, yellow, gold, orange, shades of pink and red
Height: 30 cm–1.8 m (1–6')
Spread: 30–45 cm (12–18")

Dahlia

Dahlia

The variation in size, shape and colour of dahlia flowers is astonishing. You will find at least one that appeals to you.

Growing

Dahlias prefer **full sun**. The soil should be **fertile**, rich in **organic matter, moist** and **well drained**. All dahlias are tender, tuberous perennials treated as annuals. Tubers can be purchased and started early indoors. The tubers can also be lifted in fall and stored over winter in slightly moist peat moss. Pot them and keep them in a bright room when they start sprouting in mid- to late winter. Deadhead to keep plants tidy and blooming.

Tips

Dahlias make attractive, colourful additions to a mixed border. The smaller varieties make good edging plants and the larger ones make good alternatives to shrubs. Varieties with unusual or interesting flowers are attractive specimen plants.

Recommended

Of the many dahlia hybrids, most are grown from tubers but a few can be started from seed. Many hybrids are sold based on flower shape, such as collarette, decorative or peony-flowered. The flowers range in size from 5–30 cm (2–12") and are available in many colours. Check with your local garden centre to see what is available.

In the 18th century, the first European breeders of these Mexican plants were more interested in them as a food source. The blooms were thought to be unexceptional.

Features: summer flowers, attractive foliage, bushy habit **Flower colour:** purple, pink, white, yellow, orange, red or bicoloured **Height:** 20 cm–1.5 m (8"–5') **Spread:** 20–45 cm (8–18")

Dusty Miller
Senecio

*D*usty miller makes an artful addition to planters, window boxes and mixed borders where the soft, silvery grey, deeply lobed foliage makes a good backdrop to show off the brightly coloured flowers of other annuals.

Growing
Dusty miller prefers **full sun** but tolerates light shade. The soil should be of **average fertility** and **well drained**.

Tips
The soft, silvery, lacy foliage is this plant's main feature. Dusty miller is used primarily as an edging plant, but also in beds, borders and containers.

Pinch off the flowers before they bloom. They aren't showy and they steal energy that would otherwise go to producing more foliage.

Recommended
S. cineraria forms a mound of fuzzy, silvery grey, lobed or finely divided foliage. Many cultivars have been developed with impressive foliage colours and shapes.

Features: silvery foliage, neat habit
Flower colour: yellow to cream, grown for silvery foliage **Height:** 30–60 cm (12–24")
Spread: equal to height or slightly narrower

Forget-Me-Not
Myosotis

*A*fter a long winter, the emergence of the lovely blue forget-me-not comes as a welcome sight. Though it is short lived, its habit of self-seeding each year ensures that you won't forget it.

Growing
Forget-me-not prefers **light or partial shade**, but it will tolerate full sun if the soil stays moist and the weather isn't too hot. The soil should be **fertile**, **moist** and **well drained**. Forget-me-not is a short-lived perennial that is treated like an annual. It may self-seed if faded plants are left in place until the following spring.

Tips
Forget-me-not is a delightful addition to woodland or wet areas and wildflower gardens. It can be used in the front of flowerbeds or to edge beds and borders. Try planting it in mixed containers, in rock gardens or on rock walls. This plant thrives in cooler parts of the garden.

Recommended
M. sylvatica forms a low, clustered mound of leaves. Clusters of tiny flowers with yellow centres are held on narrow, fuzzy stems above the foliage.

The common name refers to this plant's short blooming period and subsequent production of new seedlings.

Features: clusters of tiny flowers
Flower colour: blue, pink or white
Height: 15–30 cm (6–12")
Spread: 15 cm (6") or wider

Fuchsia

Fuchsia

Some gardeners who have grown fuchsias over several years have trained the plants to adopt tree forms.

These beautiful, shade-blooming plants should be grown in every garden. Our cool summer climate is perfect for growing fuchsias.

Growing

Fuchsias grow in **partial** or **light shade**. They will not tolerate summer heat, and full sun can be too hot for them. Soil should be **fertile, moist** and **well drained**. Plant them after the last frost.

Fuchsias should be deadheaded. Pluck the swollen seedpods from behind the fading petals or else the seeds will ripen and rob the plant of energy it needs for flower production.

Fuchsias bloom on new growth and prefer a plant food high in nitrogen, which encourages new growth.

Tips

Plant upright fuchsias in mixed planters, beds and borders. Pendulous fuchsias are most often used in hanging baskets, but they make attractive additions to planters and rock gardens.

Recommended

F. **Angel's Earrings Series** from Proven Winners tolerate heat and humidity.

Dozens of cultivars of *F.* x *hybrida* are available in both upright and pendulous forms. Cultivars with bronzy red foliage are also available.

Features: colourful, pendent flowers
Flower colour: pink, red, orange, purple, purple-blue or white; often bicoloured
Height: 15–90 cm (6–36")
Spread: 20–90 cm (8–36")

Gazania

Gazania

Few other flowers can rival gazania when it comes to adding vivid oranges, reds and yellows to the garden.

Growing

Gazania grows best in **full sun** but tolerates some shade. The soil should be of **poor to average fertility, sandy** and **well drained**. Gazania is drought tolerant and grows best when temperatures climb over 25° C (75° F). Flowers may only stay open on sunny days.

Tips

Low-growing gazania makes an excellent groundcover and is also useful on exposed slopes, in mixed containers and as an edging in flowerbeds. It is a wonderful plant for a xeriscape or dry garden design.

Recommended

G. rigens forms a low basal rosette of lobed foliage. Large, daisy-like flowers with pointed petals are borne on strong stems above the plant. Many cultivars are available.

This native of southern Africa has very few pests and transplants easily, even when blooming.

Features: colourful flowers
Flower colour: red, orange, yellow, pink, cream **Height:** usually 15–20 cm (6–8");
may reach 30–45 cm (12–18")
Spread: 20–30 cm (8–12")

Geranium

Pelargonium

Tough, predictable, sun-loving and drought-resistant, geraniums have earned their place as flowering favourites in the annual garden. If you are looking for something out of the ordinary, seek out the scented geraniums with their fragrant and often decorative foliage.

Growing

Geraniums prefer **full sun** but will tolerate partial shade, though they may not bloom as profusely. The soil should be **fertile** and **well drained**.

Deadheading is essential to keep geraniums blooming and looking neat.

Tips

Geraniums are very popular annual plants, used in borders, beds, planters, hanging baskets and window boxes.

Geraniums are perennials that are treated as annuals and can be kept indoors over winter in a bright room.

Recommended

P. peltatum (ivy-leaved geranium) has thick, waxy leaves and a trailing habit. Many cultivars are available.

P. zonale (zonal geranium) is a bushy plant with red, pink, purple, orange or white flowers and, frequently, banded or multi-coloured foliage. Many cultivars are available.

P. species and **cultivars** (scented geraniums, scented pelargoniums) are part of a large group of geraniums that have scented leaves. The scents are grouped into the categories of rose, mint, citrus, fruit, spice and pungent.

Ivy-leaved geranium is one of the most beautiful plants to include in a mixed hanging basket.

Features: colourful flowers, decorative or scented foliage, variable habits
Flower colour: red, pink, violet, orange, salmon, white or purple **Height:** 20–60 cm (8–24") **Spread:** 15 cm–1.2 m (6"–4')

Impatiens
Impatiens

*I*mpatiens are the high-wattage darlings of the shade garden, delivering masses of flowers in a wide variety of colours.

Growing

Impatiens do best in **partial shade** or **light shade** but tolerate full shade or, if kept moist, full sun. The soil should be **fertile, humus rich, moist** and **well drained**.

Tips

Impatiens are known for their ability to grow and flower profusely even in shade. Mass plant them in beds under trees, along shady fences or walls or in porch planters. They also look lovely in hanging baskets.

New Guinea impatiens are grown as much for their variegated leaves as for their flowers.

Recommended

I. hawkeri (New Guinea hybrids; New Guinea impatiens) flowers in shades of red, orange, pink, purple or white. The foliage is often variegated, with a yellow stripe down the centre of each leaf. This plant is the best impatiens variety for sunny locations.

I. walleriana (impatiens, busy Lizzie) flowers in shades of purple, red, burgundy, pink, yellow, salmon, orange, apricot and white and can be bicoloured. Dozens of cultivars are available.

Also called: busy Lizzie **Features:** colourful flowers, grows well in shade
Flower colour: shades of purple, red, burgundy, pink, yellow, salmon, orange, apricot, white; bicoloured **Height:** 15–90 cm (6–36") **Spread:** 30–60 cm (12–24")

The English named I. walleriana *busy Lizzie because it flowers continuously through the growing season.*

Lavatera
Lavatera

$\mathcal{L}$ avatera is great for locations with tough growing conditions. Many flowers fail in dry, infertile soil, but lavatera just keeps blooming. It only stops with the first hard frost of fall.

Growing
Lavatera prefers **full sun**. The soil should be of **average fertility, light** and **well drained**. This plant likes cool, moist weather and shelter from the wind. Use peat pots when starting seeds indoors. Lavatera resents having its roots disturbed; direct seeding is best. Plant out after last frost. Stake tall varieties to keep them from falling over during summer rain showers.

Tips
These large, shrubby plants work well in beds and borders or behind smaller plants for a colourful backdrop. Or try planting them as a temporary hedge. The flowers can be used for cutting and are edible.

Recommended
L. trimestris is a bushy plant that bears red, pink, rose pink, salmon pink or white funnel-shaped flowers. The pale pink varieties cast a silvery glow with darker pink veining from the centre to each petal's edge.

Also called: mallow **Features:** delicate flowers, easy care, tough plant
Flower colour: rose, pink, salmon or white
Height: 60 cm–1.2 m (2–4')
Spread: 45–60 cm (18–24")

Lobelia

Lobelia

Lobelia is a lovely plant that adds colour to shady spots and blends well with fuchsias and begonias. Lobelia also does well in the sun. Mix them with marigolds for a striking combination.

Growing

Lobelia grows well in **full sun** or **partial shade**, in **fertile, moist, fairly well-drained** soil high in **organic matter**. Lobelia likes cool summer nights. Ensure that its soil stays moist in hot weather. Plant out after the last frost.

Because seedlings are prone to damping off, be sure to use good, clean, seed-starting soil mix. Damping off causes plants to rot at the soil level, flop over and die.

Tips

Use lobelia along the edges of beds and borders, on rock walls, in rock gardens, mixed containers and hanging baskets.

Trim lobelia back after its first wave of flowers. This helps ensure the plant blooms through summer. In hot areas, lobelia may die back over summer, but it usually revives as the weather cools.

Recommended

L. erinus may be rounded and bushy or low and trailing. Many cultivars are available in both forms.

These lovely plants from the bellflower family contain deadly alkaloids and have poisoned people who tried to use them as herbal medicine.

Features: abundant, colourful flowers
Flower colour: purple, blue, pink, white, red **Height:** 8–23 cm (3–9")
Spread: 15 cm (6") or wider

Love-Lies-Bleeding
Amaranthus

The long, trailing flowers dry beautifully and hold their colour well.

Love-lies-bleeding forms bold, tassel-like, deep red flowers. Make sure you plant something beautiful underneath it because the flower stems point downward and observers' eyes are sure to follow.

Growing
A location in **full sun** is preferable. The soil should be **poor to average** and **well drained**. Rich soil and overfertilizing produces plants that are tall, soft and prone to falling over. Love-lies-bleeding self-seeds and may sprout up in your garden year after year. Unwanted plants are easy to uproot when they are young.

Tips
Love-lies-bleeding looks attractive grouped in borders or in mixed containers, where it requires very little care or water. It can also be planted in a large container with other colourful annuals. Its flowers will drape over the sides of the container to the ground.

Recommended
A. caudatus has long, drooping, rope-like, fluffy red, yellow or green flower spikes. A variety of other species and cultivars are available in fiery colours and different forms.

Ancient Greeks saw Amaranthus *as a symbol of fidelity and immortality. The flowers were used to decorate tombs.*

Also called: amaranth, tassel flower, velvet flower **Features:** long, tassel-like flowers
Flower colour: red, yellow, green
Height: 90 cm–1.5 m (3–5')
Spread: 45–75 cm (18–30")

Marigold
Tagetes

From the large, exotic, ruffled flowers of African marigold to the tiny flowers on the low-growing signet marigold, the warm colours and fresh scent of marigolds add a festive touch to the garden.

Growing

Marigolds grow best in **full sun**. The soil should be of **average fertility** and **well drained**. These plants are drought tolerant and hold up well in windy, rainy weather. Sow seed directly in the garden after the chance of frost has passed. Deadhead to prolong blooming and to keep plants tidy.

Tips

Mass planted or mixed with other plants, marigolds make a vibrant addition to beds, borders and container gardens. These plants will thrive in the hottest, driest parts of your garden.

Recommended

There are many cultivars available. *T. erecta* (African marigold, American marigold, Aztec marigold) is the largest plant with the biggest flowers; *T. patula* (French marigold) is low growing and comes in a wide range of flower colours; *T. tenuifolia* (signet marigold) has become more popular recently because of its feathery foliage and small, dainty flowers; *T. Triploid Hybrids* (triploid marigold), developed by crossing French and African marigolds, have huge flowers and compact growth.

Marigold is Edmonton's official flower. The warm, bright colours symbolize the city's bright sunny days and its role in the Klondike Gold Rush.

Features: brightly coloured flowers, fragrant foliage **Flower colour:** yellow, red, orange, brown, gold, cream, bicoloured **Height:** 15–90 cm (6–36") **Spread:** 30–60 cm (12–24")

Million Bells

Calibrachoa

Million bells is charming, and given the right conditions, blooms continually during the growing season.

Growing

A million bells plant prefers **full sun**. The soil should be **fertile, moist** and **well drained**. Although it prefers to be watered regularly, million bells is fairly drought resistant once established. It blooms well into autumn and it becomes hardier over summer and as the weather cools.

Tips

Popular for planters and hanging baskets, million bells is also attractive in beds and borders.

Recommended

Calibrachoa **hybrids** have dense, trailing habits. They bear small flowers that look like petunias, and cultivars are available in a wide range of flower colours.

Million bells grows all summer and needs plenty of room to spread or it will overtake other flowers. Pinch back to keep plants compact.

Also called: calibrachoa, trailing petunia **Features:** colourful flowers, trailing habit **Flower colour:** pink, purple, yellow, red-orange, white, blue **Height:** 15–30 cm (6–12") **Spread:** up to 60 cm (24")

Nasturtium
Tropaeolum

These fast-growing, brightly coloured flowers are easy to grow, making them popular with both beginners and experienced gardeners.

Growing
Nasturtiums prefer **full sun** but tolerate some shade. The soil should be of **poor to average fertility, light, moist** and **well drained**. Soil that is too rich or has too much nitrogen fertilizer will result in lots of leaves and very few flowers. Let the soil drain completely between waterings. Sow directly in the garden once the danger of frost has passed.

Tips
Nasturtiums are used in beds, borders, containers and hanging baskets and on sloped banks. The climbing varieties are grown up trellises or over rock walls or places that need concealing. These plants thrive in poor locations, and they make an interesting addition to plantings on hard-to-mow slopes.

Recommended
T. majus has a trailing habit, but many of the cultivars have bushier, more refined habits. Cultivars offer differing flower colours or variegated foliage.

The leaves and flowers are edible, and add a peppery flavour to salads.

Features: brightly coloured flowers, attractive leaves, edible leaves and flowers, varied habits
Flower colour: red, orange, yellow, burgundy, pink, cream, gold, white or bicoloured **Height:** 30–45 cm (12–18") for dwarf varieties; up to 3 m (10') for trailing varieties
Spread: equal to height

Nemesia
Nemesia

Cute as a button, this cool-season annual has snapdragon-like flowers in a variety of shades. The tall flower spikes are often used as long-lasting cut flowers.

Growing
Nemesia prefers **full sun**. The soil should be **average to fertile, slightly acidic, moist** and **well drained**. Regular watering will keep these plants blooming through the summer.

Tips
Nemesia is a bright and colourful addition to the front of a mixed border or mixed container. It may be slow to start and it may fade a bit during the hottest part of summer, but as the weather cools in late summer, nemesia will revive and start flowering once again.

Recommended
N. strumosa, a perennial that is sometimes grown as an annual, forms a bushy mound of bright green foliage. The flowers are carried high above the foliage on tall spikes. The many cultivars offer a variety of solid and bicoloured flowers including 'Bluebird' with lavender blue flowers, 'KLM' with blue and white bicoloured flowers and the **Carnival Series** with flowers in yellow, white, orange, pink or red.

Deadhead nemesia to prolong its blooming and pinch its tips when the plant is young to promote a bushy form.

Features: colourful flowers, habit
Flower colour: red, blue, purple, pink, white, yellow, orange or bicoloured
Height: 15–60 cm (6–24")
Spread: 10–30 cm (4–12")

Pansy
Viola

Pansies are one of the most popular annuals available and for good reason. They're often planted in early spring, long before any other annual, because they can tolerate frost like no other. They continue to bloom and bloom and require little care.

Growing

Pansies prefer **full sun** but tolerate partial shade. The soil should be **fertile**, **moist** and **well drained**. Pansies do best in cool weather.

Tips

Pansies can be used in beds and borders or they can be mixed with spring-flowering bulbs. They can also be grown in containers. With the varied colour combinations available, pansies complement most other types of bedding plant.

Plant a second crop of pansies late in summer to refresh tired flowerbeds well into the cool months of fall.

Recommended

V. x *wittrockiana* is available in a wide variety of solid, patterned, bicoloured and multi-coloured flowers with face-like markings in every size imaginable. The foliage is bright green and lightly scalloped along the edges.

The more you pick, the more profusely the plants will bloom, so deadhead throughout the summer months.

Also called: viola **Features:** colourful flowers **Flower colour:** blue, purple, red, orange, yellow, pink, white, multi-coloured **Height:** 8–25 cm (3–10") **Spread:** 15–30 cm (6–12")

Peekaboo Plant

Acmella (Spilanthes)

This beautiful but odd little plant lives up to its common name. Its petalless flowers resemble small eyeballs peeking out through rich foliage. Kids and adults alike will immediately love this newly introduced annual for its curious flowers and various uses.

Growing

Peekaboo plant prefers a location in **full to part sun**. The soil should be of **average fertility, moist** but **well drained**.

Tips

This unusual annual grows best in containers where it can't get lost among other plants. It can also be planted with complementary plants as an unusual accent or all by itself as a specimen.

Recommended

A. oleracea 'Peekaboo' (*Spilanthes oleracea*) is a mound-forming annual with dark, bronze purple foliage with ribbed edges. Its main attraction is its unique flowers. These petalless, round, fuzzy yellow balls have maroon centres on wiry purple stems.

This plant is still relatively new, but as an eye-catching conversation piece it's worth searching for.

Features: colourful foliage; unusual flowers; tight, mounding form
Flower colour: yellow with burgundy brown centres **Height:** 30–45 cm (12–18") **Spread:** 45–60 cm (18–24")

Petunia

Petunia

For speedy growth, prolific blooming and ease of care, petunias are hard to beat.

Growing

Petunias prefer **full sun**. The soil should be of **average to rich fertility, light, sandy** and **well drained**. Pinch halfway back in mid-summer to keep plants bushy and to encourage new growth and flowers.

Tips

Use petunias in beds, borders, containers and hanging baskets.

Recommended

P. x *hybrida* is a large group of popular, sun-loving annuals that fall into three categories: **grandifloras** have the largest flowers in the widest range of colours, but they can be damaged by rain; **multifloras** bear more flowers that are smaller and less easily damaged by heavy rain; and **millifloras** have the smallest flowers in the narrowest range of colours, but this type is the most prolific and least likely to be damaged by heavy rain.

The name petunia *is derived from* petun, *the Brazilian word for tobacco, which refers to the related genus* Nicotiana.

Features: colourful flowers, versatile plants **Flower colour:** pink, purple, red, white, yellow, coral, blue or bicoloured
Height: 15–45 cm (6–18")
Spread: 30–60 cm (12–24") or wider

Salvia
Salvia

The genus name Salvia *comes from the Latin* salvus, *which means 'safe' or 'healed.' This refers to the medicinal properties of several species.*

Salvias should be part of every annual garden. There are over 900 species of *Salvia,* and the attractive and varied forms have something to offer every style of garden.

Growing

All salvia plants prefer **full sun** but tolerate light shade. The soil should be **moist, well drained** and of **average to rich fertility** with lots of **organic matter.**

Tips

Salvias look good grouped in beds and borders and in containers. The flowers are long lasting and make good cut flowers for arrangements.

To keep plants producing flowers, water often and fertilize monthly.

Recommended

S. argentea (silver sage) is grown for its large, fuzzy, silvery leaves. *S. coccinea* (Texas sage) is a bushy, upright plant that bears whorled spikes of white, pink, blue or purple flowers. *S. farinacea* (mealy cup sage, blue sage) has bright blue flowers clustered along stems powdered with silver. Cultivars are available. *S. splendens* (salvia, scarlet sage) is grown for its spikes of bright red, tubular flowers. Recently, cultivars have become available in white, pink, purple and orange. *S. viridis* (*S. horminium,* annual clary sage) is grown for its colourful pink, purple, blue or white bracts, not its flowers.

***

Also called: sage **Features:** colourful summer flowers, attractive foliage
Flower colour: red, blue, purple, burgundy, pink, orange, salmon, yellow, cream, white or bicoloured **Height:** 20 cm–1.2 m (8"–4')
Spread: 20 cm–1.2 m (8"–4')

Snapdragon
Antirrhinum

Snapdragons are among the most appealing plants. The flower colours are always rich and vibrant, and even the most jaded gardeners are tempted to squeeze open the dragons' mouths.

Growing
Snapdragons prefer **full sun** but tolerate light or partial shade. The soil should be **fertile, rich in organic matter** and **well drained**. These plants prefer a **neutral or alkaline** soil and will not perform as well in acidic soil. Do not cover seeds when sowing because they require light for germination.

To encourage bushy growth, pinch the tips of the young plants. Cut off the flower spikes as they fade to promote further blooming and to prevent the plant from dying back before the end of the season.

Tips
The height of the variety dictates the best place for it in a border—shorter varieties work well near the front, and the tallest look good in the centre or back. The dwarf and medium-height varieties can also be used in planters. Try planting trailing varieties in hanging baskets.

Recommended
The many cultivars of **A. majus** are generally grouped into three size categories: dwarf, medium and giant.

Snapdragons can handle cold weather, so they are a good choice for gardeners who can't wait until the last frost date to plant their annuals.

Features: entertaining summer flowers
Flower colour: white, cream, yellow, orange, red, maroon, pink, purple or bicoloured **Height:** 15 cm–1.2 m (6"–4')
Spread: 15–60 cm (6–24")

Sweet Alyssum
Lobularia

Sweet alyssum is excellent for creating soft edges, and it self-seeds, popping up along pathways and between stones late in the season to give summer a sweet send-off.

Growing

Sweet alyssum prefers **full sun** but tolerates light shade. **Well-drained** soil of **average fertility** is preferred, but poor soil is tolerated. Sweet alyssum may die back a bit during the heat and humidity of summer. Trim it back and water it periodically to encourage new growth and more flowers when the weather cools.

Tips

Sweet alyssum creeps around rock gardens, over rock walls and along the edges of beds. It is an excellent choice for seeding into cracks and crevices of walkways and between patio stones, and once established it readily reseeds. It is also good for filling in spaces between taller plants in borders and mixed containers.

Recommended

L. maritima forms a low, spreading mound of foliage. The entire plant appears to be covered in tiny blossoms when in full flower. Cultivars with flowers in a wide range of colours are available.

Leave alyssum plants out all winter. In spring, remove the previous year's growth to expose self-sown seedlings below.

Features: fragrant flowers
Flower colour: pink, purple, yellow, salmon, white **Height:** 8–30 cm (3–12") **Spread:** 15–60 cm (6–24")

Sweet Potato Vine

Ipomoea

This vigorous rambling plant, with its lime green, bruised purple or green, pink and cream variegated leaves can make any gardener look like a genius.

Growing

Grow sweet potato vine in **full sun**. Any type of soil will do, but a **light, well-drained** soil of **poor fertility** is preferred.

Tips

Sweet potato vine is a great addition to mixed planters, window boxes and hanging baskets. In a rock garden it will scramble about, and when planted along the top of a retaining wall it will cascade over the edge.

Recommended

I. batatas (sweet potato vine) is a twining climber that is grown for its attractive foliage rather than its flowers. Several cultivars are available.

As a bonus, when you pull up your plant at the end of summer, you can eat any tubers (sweet potatoes) that have formed.

Features: decorative foliage
Flower colour: grown for foliage
Height: about 30 cm (12")
Spread: up to 3 m (10')

Verbena
Verbena

Verbenas offer butterflies a banquet. Butterfly visitors include tiger swallowtails, silver-spotted skippers, great spangled fritillaries and painted ladies.

The Romans, it is said, believed verbena could rekindle the flames of dying love. They named it Herba Veneris, *'plant of Venus.'*

Growing

Verbenas grow best in **full sun**. The soil should be **fertile** and **very well drained**. Pinch back young plants for bushy growth.

Tips

Use verbenas on rock walls and in beds, borders, rock gardens, containers, hanging baskets and window boxes. They make good substitutes for ivy-leaved geraniums where the sun is hot and where a roof overhang keeps the mildew-prone verbenas dry.

Recommended

V. bonariensis forms a low clump of foliage from which tall, stiff stems bear clusters of small, purple flowers.

V. x *hybrida* is a bushy plant that may be upright or spreading. It bears clusters of small flowers in a wide range of colours. Cultivars are available.

Also called: garden verbena **Features:** summer flowers **Flower colour:** red, pink, purple, blue, yellow, scarlet, silver, peach or white; some with white centres **Height:** 20 cm–1.5 m (8"–5') **Spread:** 30–90 cm (12–36")

Artemisia

Artemisia

Most artemisias are valued for their silvery foliage, not their flowers. Silver is the ultimate blending colour in the garden because it enhances every other hue.

Growing

Artemisias grow best in **full sun** with **well-drained** soil of **low to average fertility**. These plants dislike wet, humid conditions.

Artemisias respond well to pruning in late spring. If you prune before May, frost may kill any new growth. When artemisias begin to look straggly, cut them back hard to encourage new growth and maintain a neater form. Divide them every year or two, when plants appear to be thinning in the centres.

Tips

Use artemisias in rock gardens and borders. Their silvery grey foliage makes them good backdrop plants for brightly coloured flowers and for filling in spaces between other plants. Smaller forms may be used to create knot gardens.

Recommended

A. ludoviciana (white sage, silver sage) is an upright, clump-forming plant with silvery white foliage. The species is not grown as often as its cultivars. (Zones 4–8)

A. schmidtiana (silvermound artemisia) is a low, dense, mound-forming perennial with feathery, hairy, silvery grey foliage. 'Nana' (dwarf silvermound) is very compact and grows only half the size of the species.

A. stelleriana (silver brocade) is a low-growing, compact variety. The silvery, scalloped foliage closely resembles that of dusty miller.

Also called: wormwood, sage Features: silvery grey, feathery or deeply lobed foliage
Flower colour: plant grown for foliage
Height: 15–90 cm (6–36") Spread: 30–90 cm (12–36") Hardiness: zones 2–8

Basket-of-Gold
Aurinia

When spring is still cool and most plants are just beginning to peek out of the soil, this electric yellow perennial comes into full bloom to warm us up.

Growing
Basket-of-gold prefers **full sun**. Soil should be of **average to poor fertility, sandy** and **well drained**. Basket-of-gold can rot in wet soil, and growth becomes floppy in rich soil.

Shear basket-of-gold back lightly after flowering. This will keep the plant compact and occasionally encourages a few more flowers. Established plants should not be moved or divided.

Tips
Use basket-of-gold in borders and rock gardens, along wall tops and as a groundcover in difficult or little-used areas.

Combine basket-of-gold with vigorous rock garden plants and spring bulbs such as tulips, but avoid planting it with slow-growing plants because it can quickly overwhelm them.

Recommended
A. saxatilis is a vigorous, mound-forming perennial. It bears bright yellow flowers in mid-spring. 'Citrina' bears light, lemon yellow flowers. 'Compacta' bears golden flowers. 'Dudley Nevill' bears apricot-coloured flowers. 'Gold Ball' is a clump-forming plant with bright yellow flowers held above the foliage. 'Variegata' bears lemon yellow flowers and has irregular, cream-coloured margins on the foliage.

Features: flowers, form Flower colour: yellow, gold Height: 15–45 cm (6–18") Spread: 20–45 cm (8–18") Hardiness: zones 3–8

Bellflower

Campanula

Thanks to their wide range of heights and habits, it is possible to put bellflowers almost anywhere in the garden.

Growing

Bellflowers grow well in **full sun, partial shade** or **light shade**. The soil should be of **average to high fertility** and **well drained**. Mulch to keep roots cool and moist in summer and protected in winter, particularly if snow cover is inconsistent. Deadhead to prolong blooming.

Tips

Plant upright and mounding bellflowers in borders and cottage gardens. Use low, spreading and trailing bellflowers in rock gardens and on rock walls. You can also edge beds with the low-growing varieties.

Recommended

C. x 'Birch Hybrid' is a low-growing and spreading plant. It bears light blue to mauve flowers in summer.

C. carpatica (Carpathian bellflower, Carpathian harebell) is a spreading, mounding perennial that bears blue, white or purple flowers in summer. Several cultivars are available.

C. glomerata (clustered bellflower) forms a clump of upright stems and bears clusters of purple, blue or white flowers most of the summer.

C. persicifolia (peach-leaved bellflower) is an upright perennial that bears white, blue or purple flowers from early summer to mid-summer.

C. poscharskyana (Serbian bellflower) is a trailing perennial that winds around other plants. It bears light violet blue flowers in summer and early autumn.

Divide bellflowers every few years, in early spring or late summer, to keep plants vigorous and to prevent them from becoming invasive.

Features: spring, summer or autumn flowers; varied growing habits **Flower colour:** blue, white, purple, pink **Height:** 10–90 cm (4–36") **Spread:** 30–24 cm (12–24") **Hardiness:** zones 2–7

Black-Eyed Susan
Rudbeckia

Black-eyed Susan is a tough, low-maintenance, long-lived perennial. Plant it wherever you want a casual look. Black-eyed Susan looks great in drifts.

Growing

Black-eyed Susans grow well in **full sun** or **partial shade**. The soil should be of **average fertility** and **well drained**. Several *Rudbeckia* species are touted as 'clay-busters' for their tolerance of fairly heavy clay soils. Established plants are drought tolerant but regular watering is best. Divide in spring or fall, every three to five years.

Tips

Include these native plants in wildflower and natural gardens, beds and borders. Pinching the plants in June will result in shorter, bushier stands.

Recommended

R. fulgida, an upright, spreading plant with orange-yellow flowers with brown centres. Var. *sullivantii* 'Goldsturm' bears large, bright, golden yellow flowers.

R. laciniata (cutleaf coneflower) forms a large, open clump. The yellow flowers have green centres. **'Goldquelle'** has bright yellow, double flowers.

R. nitida is an upright, spreading plant with green-centred yellow flowers. 'Herbstsonne' ('Autumn Sun') has bright, golden yellow flowers.

The flowers last well when cut for arrangements.

Features: bright flowers, attractive foliage, easy to grow **Flower colour:** yellow, orange or red; centres typically brown or green **Height:** 60 cm–1.8 m (2–6') **Spread:** 45–90 cm (18–36") **Hardiness:** zones 3–8

Bleeding Heart

Dicentra

Every garden should have a spot for the bleeding heart. Tucked away in a shady spot, this lovely plant appears in spring and fills the garden with fresh promise.

Growing

Bleeding hearts prefer **light shade** but tolerate partial or full shade. The soil should be **humus rich, moist** and **well drained**. These plants die back in very dry summers but revive in autumn or the following spring. Bleeding hearts must remain moist while blooming to prolong the flowering period. Regular watering will keep the flowers coming until mid-summer.

D. exima and *D. spectabilis* rarely need dividing. *D. formosa* can be divided every three years or so.

Tips

Bleeding hearts can be naturalized in a woodland garden or grown in a border or rock garden. They make excellent early-season specimen plants and do well near ponds or streams.

All bleeding hearts contain toxic alkaloids, and some people develop allergic skin reactions from contact with these plants.

Recommended

D. eximia (fringed bleeding heart) forms a loose, mounded clump of lacy, fern-like foliage and bears pink or white flowers in spring and sporadically over summer.

D. formosa (western bleeding heart) is a low-growing, wide-spreading plant with pink flowers that fade to white as they mature. The most drought tolerant of the bleeding hearts, it is the most likely to continue flowering all summer.

D. spectabilis (common bleeding heart, Japanese bleeding heart) forms a large, elegant mound that bears flowers with white inner petals and pink outer petals. Several cultivars are available.

Features: spring and summer flowers, attractive foliage **Flower colour:** pink, white, red, purple
Height: 20–90 cm (8–36") **Spread:** 30–60 cm (12–24") **Hardiness:** zones 2–8

Bugbane
Cimicifuga

C. racemosa is also known as black cohosh, and the rhizomes are used in herbal medicine.

Bugbanes put on impressive displays. These tall plants bear fragrant flowers above decorative foliage.

Growing

Bugbanes grow best in **partial or light shade**. The soil should be **fertile, humus rich** and **moist**. The plants may require support from a peony hoop. Bugbanes spread by rhizomes; small pieces of root can be carefully unearthed and replanted in spring if more plants are desired.

Tips

Bugbanes make attractive additions to an open woodland garden, shaded border or pondside planting. They don't compete well with tree roots or other plants that have vigorous roots. Bugbanes are worth growing close to the house because the late-season flowers are wonderfully fragrant.

Recommended

C. racemosa (black snakeroot) is a clump-forming perennial with long-stemmed spikes of fragrant, creamy white flowers. (Zones 3–8)

C. ramosa 'Atropurpurea' (purple leaf bugbane) produces a clump of dark purple, lacy foliage topped with tall, creamy white flower spikes. **'Brunette'** has even darker foliage and pale pink flowers. (Zones 4–8)

C. simplex (Kamchatka bugbane) is a clump-forming perennial with fragrant bottlebrush-like spikes of flowers. Several cultivars are available, including those with bronze or purple foliage. (Zones 3–8)

Also called: snakeroot **Features:** fragrant, late-summer and autumn flowers, some with bronze or purple foliage **Flower colour:** white, cream, pink **Height:** 60 cm–1.5 m (2–5') **Spread:** 60 cm–90 cm (2–3') **Hardiness:** zones 3–8

Coral Bells

Heuchera

From soft yellow-greens and oranges to midnight purples and silvery, dappled maroons, coral bells offer a great variety of foliage options for a perennial garden with partial shade.

Growing

Coral bells grow best in **light or partial shade**. The foliage colours can bleach out in full sun, and plants grow leggy in full shade. The soil should be of **average to rich fertility, humus rich, neutral to alkaline, moist** and **well drained**. Good air circulation is essential. Deadhead to prolong the bloom. Every two or three years, coral bells should be dug up and the oldest, woodiest roots and stems removed. Plants may be divided at this time, if desired, then replanted with the crown at or just above soil level.

Tips

Use coral bells as edging plants, in clusters and woodland gardens or as groundcovers in low-traffic areas. Combine different foliage types for an interesting display.

Recommended

There are dozens of beautiful cultivars available with almost limitless variations of foliage markings and colours. See your local garden centre or mail-order catalogue for availability.

Coral bells have a strange habit of pushing themselves up out of the soil because of their shallow root systems. Mulch in autumn if the plants begin heaving from the ground.

Also called: heuchera, alum root
Features: very decorative foliage, spring or summer flowers **Flower colour:** red, pink, white, yellow, purple; plant also grown for foliage.
Height: 30–75 cm (12–30") **Spread:** 15–45 cm (6–18") **Hardiness:** zones 3–8

Daylily
Hemerocallis

The daylily's adaptability and durability combined with its variety in colour, blooming period, size and texture explain this perennial's popularity.

Growing

Daylilies grow in any light from **full sun to full shade**. The deeper the shade, the fewer flowers will be produced. The soil should be **fertile, moist** and **well drained**, but these plants adapt to most conditions and are hard to kill once established. Divide every two to three years to keep plants vigorous and to propagate them. They can, however, be left indefinitely without dividing.

Tips

Plant daylilies alone, or group them in borders, on banks and in ditches to control erosion. They can be naturalized in woodland or meadow gardens. Small varieties look nice in planters.

Deadhead to prolong the blooming period. Be careful when deadheading purple-flowered daylilies because the sap can stain fingers and clothes.

Recommended

Daylilies come in an almost infinite number of forms, sizes and colours in a range of species, cultivars and hybrids. See your local garden centre or daylily grower to find out what's available and most suitable for your garden.

Features: spring and summer flowers, grass-like foliage **Flower colour:** comes in every colour except blue and pure white **Height:** 30 cm–1.2 m (1–4') **Spread:** 30 cm–1.2 m (1–4') **Hardiness:** zones 2–8

Dead Nettle
Lamium

These attractive plants, with their striped, dotted or banded silver and green foliage, hug the ground and thrive on only the barest necessities of life.

Growing

Dead nettles prefer **partial to light shade**. They tolerate full sun but may become leggy. The soil should be of **average fertility, humus rich, moist** and **well drained**. The more fertile the soil, the more vigorously the plants will grow. They are drought tolerant in shade but develop bare patches if the soil dries out for extended periods. Divide and replant in autumn if bare spots become unsightly.

Dead nettles remain more compact if sheared back after flowering. If they remain green over winter, shear them back in early spring.

Dead nettle's lime green leaves offset darker colours.

Tips

These plants make useful groundcovers for woodland or shade gardens. They also help keep weeds down under shrubs in a border.

Recommended

L. galeobdolon (*Lamiastrum galeobdolon*; yellow archangel) can be invasive, though the cultivars are less so. The yellow flowers bloom in spring to early summer. Several cultivars are available.

L. maculatum (spotted dead nettle) is the most commonly grown dead nettle. This low-growing, spreading species has green leaves with white or silvery markings and bears white, pink or mauve flowers. Many cultivars are available.

Also called: spotted dead nettle, lamium, yellow archangel **Features:** spring or summer flowers; decorative, often variegated foliage **Flower colour:** white, pink, yellow, mauve; plant also grown for foliage **Height:** 15–60 cm (6–24") **Spread:** 30–60 cm (12–24") **Hardiness:** zones 2–8

Delphinium
Delphinium

*D*elphinium is the royalty of the perennial border. Tall, bold and astounding in bloom, delphinium reminds us what growing flowers is all about.

Growing

Grow delphiniums in a **full sun** location that is well protected from strong winds. Soil should be **fertile**, **moist** and **humus rich** with **excellent drainage**.

Tips

Delphiniums are classic cottage garden plants. Their height and need for staking relegate them to the back of the border where they make a nice backdrop for foreground flowers such as peonies, poppies and black-eyed Susans.

Recommended

D. x *belladonna* (belladonna hybrids) bear flowers of blue, white or mauve in loose, branched spikes. They grow over 1 m tall and almost 60 cm wide.

D. x *elatum* (elatum hybrids) bear dense clusters of blue, purple, white, pink or yellow flowers on tall spikes. They are divided into three height categories—dwarfs, mediums and talls—ranging in height from 1.6 to 2 m (5–6½') tall.

D. grandiflorum bears flowers of blue, purple or white in loose, branched clusters. It grows 60 cm (24") tall and 30 cm (12") wide.

Features: tall, spiky clusters of colourful flowers and ornate foliage
Flower colour: blue, purple, pink, white or bicoloured **Height:** 60 cm–2 m (2–6½') **Spread:** 30–100 cm (12–40") **Hardiness:** zones 3–7

Elephant Ears
Bergenia

The reawakening of elephant ears is a sure sign of spring. The leaves only fade and collapse a little throughout the winter months but once the snow melts in spring, they rise up, take shape and bloom.

Growing

Elephant ears grows best in **partial shade**. The soil should be of **average to rich fertility** and **well drained**. A moist soil is preferable, especially when plants are grown in sunnier areas. However, elephant ears is fairly drought tolerant once established.

Tips

These versatile, low-growing, spreading plants can be used as groundcovers, as edging along borders and pathways, as part of woodland rock gardens and in mass plantings under trees and shrubs.

Recommended

B. cordifolia (heart-leaved bergenia) produces rounded, leathery foliage in dense clusters. The leaves turn a reddish shade of bronze in the fall. Purplish flower stems rise through the foliage tipped with clusters of pink flowers in early spring. Cultivars are available with varied flower and foliage colour.

B. cordifolia *has several common names, including pigsqueak, giant rockfoil, heart-leaf bergenia and leather-leaf rockfoil.*

Also called: bergenia **Features:** evergreen foliage and complementary flowers **Flower colour:** red, purple, light to dark pink, white **Height:** 60 cm (24") **Spread:** 60 cm (24") or more **Hardiness:** zones 3–8

Geranium
Geranium

There is a type of geranium that suits every garden, thanks to the beauty and diversity of this hardy plant.

Growing

Hardy geraniums dislike hot weather but grow well in **full sun, partial shade** and **light shade.** They prefer soil of **average fertility** with **good drainage.** *G. renardii* prefers a poor, well-drained soil. Divide in spring.

Tips

These long-flowering plants are great in a border; they fill in the spaces between shrubs and other larger plants, and keep the weeds down. They can be included in rock gardens and woodland gardens, or mass planted as groundcovers.

Recommended

G. 'Brookside' is a clump-forming, drought-tolerant geranium with finely cut leaves and deep blue to violet blue flowers. (Zones 4–8)

G. macrorrhizum (bigroot geranium, scented cranesbill) forms a spreading mound of fragrant foliage and bears flowers in various shades of pink. Cultivars are available. (Zones 2–8)

G. renardii (Renard's geranium) forms a clump of velvety, deeply veined, crinkled foliage. A few purple-veined white flowers appear over the summer, but the foliage remains the main attraction. (Zones 4–8)

G. sanguineum (bloodred cranesbill, bloody cranesbill) forms a dense, mounding clump and bears bright magenta flowers. Many cultivars are available. (Zones 3–8)

Also called: cranesbill geranium **Features:** summer flowers; attractive, sometimes fragrant foliage **Flower colour:** white, red, pink, purple, blue **Height:** 10–45 cm (4–18") **Spread:** 30–60 cm (12–24") **Hardiness:** zones 2–8

Goat's Beard

Aruncus

Despite its imposing size, goat's beard has a soft and delicate appearance with its divided foliage and large, plumy, cream flowers.

Growing

These plants prefer **partial to full shade**. If planted in deep shade, they bear fewer blooms. They will tolerate some full sun as long as the soil is kept evenly moist and they are protected from the afternoon sun. The soil should be **fertile, moist** and **humus rich**.

Divide in spring or autumn. Use a sharp knife or an axe to cut the dense root mass into pieces. Fortunately, these plants rarely need dividing.

Tips

These plants look very natural growing near the sunny entrance or edge of a woodland garden, in a native plant garden or in a large island planting. They may also be used in a border or alongside a stream or pond.

Recommended

A. aethusifolius (dwarf Korean goat's beard) forms a low-growing, compact mound and bears branched spikes of loosely held, cream flowers.

A. dioicus (giant goat's beard, common goat's beard) forms a large, bushy, shrub-like perennial with large plumes of creamy white flowers. There are several cultivars.

Male and female flowers are produced on separate plants. Male flowers are full and fuzzy while female flowers are more pendulous.

Features: early- to mid-summer blooms, shrub-like habit, attractive foliage and seedheads
Flower colour: cream, white **Height:** 15 cm–1.8 m (6"–6') **Spread:** 30 cm–1.2 m (12"–4') **Hardiness:** zones 2–8

Hosta

Hosta

Breeders are always looking for new variations in hosta foliage. Swirls, stripes, puckers and ribs enhance the leaves' various sizes, shapes and colours. Sun-loving hostas have recently become the new rage.

Slugs can cause unsightly damage to the beautiful foliage. If they are a problem, select "slug resistant" varieties with thick and waxy leaves that are difficult for these creatures to feed upon.

Growing

Hostas prefer **light or partial shade** but will grow in full shade. Morning sun is preferable to afternoon sun in partial shade situations. The soil should ideally be **fertile, moist** and **well drained**, but most soils are tolerated. Hostas are fairly drought tolerant, especially if given a mulch to help retain moisture.

Division is not required but can be done every few years in spring or summer to propagate new plants.

Tips

Hostas make wonderful woodland plants and look very attractive when combined with ferns and other fine-textured plants. Hostas are also good plants for a mixed border, particularly when used to hide the ugly, leggy lower stems and branches of some shrubs. Hostas' dense growth and thick, shade-providing leaves allow them to suppress weeds.

Recommended

Hostas have been subjected to a great deal of crossbreeding and hybridizing, resulting in hundreds of cultivars. Visit your local garden centre or get a mail-order catalogue to find out what's available.

Also called: plantain lily **Features:** decorative foliage, summer and autumn flowers **Flower colour:** white or purple plants grown mainly for foliage **Height:** 10–90 cm (4–36") **Spread:** 15 cm–1.8 m (6"–6') **Hardiness:** zones 2–8

Iris
Iris

Irises are steeped in history and lore. Many say the range in flower colours of bearded irises approximates that of a rainbow.

Growing

Irises prefer **full sun** but tolerate very light or dappled shade. The soil should be of **average fertility** and **well drained**. Japanese iris and Siberian iris prefer a moist but still well-drained soil.

Divide in late summer or early autumn. When dividing bearded iris rhizomes, replant with the flat side of the foliage fan facing the garden. Dust the toe-shaped rhizome with a powder cleanser before planting to help prevent soft rot.

Deadhead irises to keep them tidy. Cut back the foliage of Siberian iris in spring or fall along with your other perennials.

Tips

Irises are popular border plants; plant Japanese iris and Siberian iris alongside streams or ponds. Dwarf cultivars are attractive in rock gardens.

Wash your hands after handling irises because they can cause severe internal irritation if ingested. Do not plant them close to children's play areas.

Recommended

Among the most popular of the many species and hybrids is the bearded iris, often a hybrid of *I. germanica*. It has the widest range of flower colours, but is susceptible to the iris borer, which can kill a plant. Several irises are not susceptible, including Japanese iris (*I. ensata*), dwarf bearded iris (*I. x pumila*) and Siberian iris (*I. siberica*).

Features: spring, summer and sometimes autumn flowers; attractive foliage **Flower colour:** many shades of pink, red, purple, blue, white, brown, yellow **Height:** 20 cm–1.2 m (8"–4') **Spread:** 15 cm–1.2 m (6"–4') **Hardiness:** zones 2–8

Japanese Spurge
Pachysandra

In a slightly protected location, Japanese spurge will flourish and spread into a glossy mat of ornate foliage. Variegated varieties with white- and silvery-edged leaves are also available.

Growing

Japanese spurge prefers **light to full shade** and tolerates partial shade. Any soil that is **moist**, **acidic**, **humus rich** and **well drained** is good. The foliage is considered ever-green but can look tired by spring. Trim out tired or dead foliage to make way for new foliage in the spring.

Tips

Japanese spurge makes a durable groundcover under trees, along north walls, in shady borders and in woodland gardens.

Recommended

P. terminalis forms a low mass of glossy foliage rosettes. Its white, inconspicuous flowers appear only briefly in the spring.

Features: glossy, ornate, evergreen foliage; habit
Flower colour: white, inconspicuous **Height:** about 20 cm (8") **Spread:** 30–45 cm (12–18") or more
Hardiness: zones 4–8

Lady's Mantle
Alchemilla

Few other perennials are as captivating as lady's mantle when it's dappled with morning dew. The fine-haired leaves capture water, creating pearly drops that cling to the edges of the leaves.

Growing

Lady's mantle plants prefer **light** or **partial shade**, with protection from the afternoon sun. They dislike hot locations, and excessive sun will scorch the leaves. The soil should be **fertile**, **humus rich**, **moist** and **well drained**. These plants are drought resistant once established. Deadhead to keep the plants tidy and possibly encourage a second flush of flowers in late summer or fall.

Tips

Lady's mantle is ideal for grouping under trees in woodland gardens and along border edges. It softens the bright colours of other plants. It is also attractive in containers.

Recommended

A. mollis forms a mound of soft, rounded foliage and produces sprays of frothy-looking, yellowish green flowers in early summer.

Alchemists in the Middle Ages thought the dew captured in the centre of a lady's mantle leaf could change lead into gold.

Features: round, fuzzy leaves and tiny, chartreuse flowers
Flower colour: yellow, green
Height: 20–45 cm (8–18")
Spread: 50–60 cm (20–24")
Hardiness: zones 3–8

Lamb's Ears

Stachys

Lamb's ears' soft, fuzzy leaves give this perennial its common names. The silvery foliage is a beautiful contrast to bold-coloured plants that tower above, and it softens hard lines and surfaces.

Growing

Lamb's ears grows best in **full sun**. The soil should be of **poor** to **average fertility** and **well drained**. The leaves can rot in humid weather if the soil is poorly drained. Remove spent flower spikes to keep plants looking neat.

Tips

Lamb's ears makes a great groundcover in a new garden where the soil has not yet been amended. It can be used to edge borders and pathways because it provides a soft, silvery backdrop for more vibrant colours in the border. For a silvery accent, plant a small group of lamb's ears in a border.

Recommended

S. byzantina forms a mat of thick, woolly rosettes of leaves. Pinkish purple flowers bloom all summer. There are many cultivars that offer a variety of foliage colours, sizes and flowers.

Many plants in the mint family contain antibacterial and antifungal compounds. Lamb's ears not only feels soft but may actually encourage healing.

Also called: lamb's tails, lamb's tongues **Features:** soft and fuzzy, silver foliage **Flower colour:** pink, purple **Height:** 15–45 cm (6–18") **Spread:** 45–60 cm (18–24") **Hardiness:** zones 3–8

Ligularia
Ligularia

Ligularias are stunning plants, but only in areas where they receive adequate moisture and protection from afternoon sun. The foliage and flowers are truly unforgettable.

Growing

Ligularias should be grown in **light shade** or **partial shade** with protection from the afternoon sun. They will thrive in full sun, but only with consistently moist soil. Soil should be of **average fertility**, **humus rich** and **moist**.

Tips

Plant ligularias alongside a pond or stream. They can also be used in a well-watered border or bog garden, or naturalized in a moist meadow or woodland garden.

Recommended

L. dentata (bigleaf ligularia, golden groundsel) forms a clump of rounded, heart-shaped leaves and bears clusters of orange-yellow, daisy-like flowers. Cultivars are available in varied sizes and colours.

L. stenocephala (narrow-spiked ligularia) has toothed foliage and bears bright yellow flowers on dark, purple-green spikes.

The foliage can wilt in hot sun, even in moist soil. The leaves will revive overnight, but it is best to move the plant to a cooler, more shaded position in the garden.

Features: bright yellow flowers and ornate foliage
Flower colour: yellow or orange
Height: 90 cm–1.8 m (3–6') **Spread:** 60 cm–1.5 m (2–5')
Hardiness: zones 3–8

Lungwort
Pulmonaria

The wide array of lungworts have highly attractive foliage ranging in colour from apple green to silver-spotted, olive to dark emerald.

Growing

Lungworts prefer **partial to full shade.** The soil should be **fertile, humus rich, moist** and **well drained**. Rot can occur in very wet soil.

Divide in early summer after flowering or in autumn. Provide the newly planted divisions with lots of water to help them re-establish.

Tips

Lungworts make attractive groundcovers for shady borders, woodland gardens and pond and stream edges.

Recommended

P. longifolia (long-leaved lungwort) forms a dense clump of long, narrow, white-spotted green leaves and bears clusters of blue flowers.

P. officinalis (common lungwort, spotted dog) forms a loose clump of evergreen foliage, spotted with white. The flowers open pink and mature to blue. Cultivars are available.

P. saccharata (Bethlehem sage) forms a compact clump of large, white-spotted, evergreen leaves and purple, red or white flowers. Many cultivars are available.

To keep lungworts tidy and show off the fabulous foliage, deadhead the plants by shearing them back lightly after they flower.

Features: decorative mottled foliage, spring flowers **Flower colour:** blue, red, pink, white; plants also grown for foliage **Height:** 25–45 cm (10–18") **Spread:** 20–90 cm (8–36") **Hardiness:** zones 3–8

Meadowsweet

Filipendula

For an impressive, informal, vertical accent and clusters of fluffy, fragrant flowers, meadowsweet plants are second to none.

Growing

Meadowsweets prefer **partial or light shade**, but tolerate full sun if the soil remains sufficiently moist. The soil should be **fertile, deep, humus rich** and **moist**, except in the case of *F. vulgaris*, which prefers dry soil. Divide in spring or autumn.

Tips

Most meadowsweets are excellent plants for bog gardens or wet sites. Grow them alongside streams or in moist meadows. Meadowsweets may also be grown at the back of a border, as long as they are kept well watered. Grow *F. vulgaris* if you can't provide the moisture needed by the other species.

Recommended

F. rubra (queen-of-the-prairie) forms a large, spreading clump and bears clusters of fragrant, pink flowers. Cultivars are available.

F. ulmaria (queen-of-the-meadow) forms a mounding clump and bears creamy white flowers in large clusters. Cultivars are available.

F. vulgaris (dropwort, meadowsweet) is a low-growing species that bears clusters of fragrant, creamy white flowers. Cultivars with double or pink flowers or variegated foliage are available.

Deadhead meadowsweets if you so desire, but the faded seedheads are quite attractive when left in place.

Features: late-spring or summer flowers, attractive foliage **Flower colour:** white, cream, pink, red **Height:** 60 cm–1.8 m (12"–6') **Spread:** 30 cm–1.2 m (12"–4') **Hardiness:** zones 2–8

Pasqueflower
Pulsatilla

Pasqueflower is harmful if eaten, and repeated handling may cause skin irritation.

This plant is one of the first to bloom in spring. Its flowers often unfold beneath the last patches of snow.

Growing

Pasqueflower grows well in **full sun** or **partial shade**. The soil should be **fertile** and **very well drained**. Poorly drained, wet soil can quickly kill this plant. Pasque-flower resents being disturbed; plant it while it is very small, and don't divide it.

Tips

Pasqueflower can be grown in rock gardens, woodland gardens and borders and on gravelly banks. It also works well in pots and planters but it should be moved to a sheltered location for winter. An unheated garage or porch will offer some protection from the freeze-thaw cycles and excessive moisture of winter. Make sure the pots get some light once the plants begin to grow.

Recommended

P. vulgaris (*Anemone pulsatilla*) forms a mound of lacy foliage and bears flowers in shades of blue, purple or occasionally white. The fluffy seedheads provide interest when the flowers are gone.

Features: early- to mid-spring flowers, fluffy seedheads, attractive foliage **Flower colour:** purple, blue, red, white **Height:** 10–30 cm (4–12") **Spread:** 20–30 cm (8–12") **Hardiness:** zones 2–8

Peony

Paeonia

Once the fleeting but magnificent peony flower display is done, the foliage remains stellar throughout the growing season.

Growing

Peonies prefer **full sun** but tolerate some shade. The planting site should be well prepared with **fertile, humus-rich, moist, well-drained** soil and lots of compost. Mulch peonies lightly with compost in spring. Too much fertilizer, particularly nitrogen, causes floppy growth and retards blooming. Division is not required, but can be done in autumn to propagate plants. Deadhead to keep plants looking tidy.

Tips

Peonies look great in a border combined with other early bloomers. They may be underplanted with bulbs—when the other plants die down by mid-summer, the emerging peony foliage will hide the dying foliage. Avoid planting peonies under trees, where they will have to compete for moisture and nutrients.

Tubers planted too shallow or, more commonly, too deep will not flower. The buds or eyes on the tuber should be planted 3–5 cm (1–2") below the soil surface.

Place wire tomato or peony cages around the plants in early spring to support the heavy flowers. The foliage will grow into the wires and hide the cage.

Recommended

There are hundreds of peonies available. Cultivars come in a wide range of colours, may have single or double flowers and may or may not be fragrant. Visit your local garden centre for availability.

Features: spring and early-summer flowers, attractive foliage **Flower colour:** white, cream white, yellow, pink, red, purple **Height:** 60–80 cm (24–32") **Spread:** 60–80 cm (24–32") **Hardiness:** zones 2–8

Phlox

Phlox

Phlox comes in many shapes and sizes, from low creepers to bushy border plants. Its flowering periods fall anywhere between early spring and mid-autumn.

Growing

P. paniculata and *P. maculata* prefer **full sun**; *P. subulata* prefers **full sun to partial shade**; and *P. stolonifera* prefers **light to partial shade** but tolerates heavy shade. All like **fertile, humus rich, moist, well-drained** soil. Divide in autumn or spring.

Tips

Low-growing species are useful in rock gardens or at the front of borders. Taller phloxes may be used in the middle of borders and are particularly effective if planted in groups.

Recommended

P. maculata (early phlox, garden phlox, wild sweet William) forms an upright clump of hairy stems and narrow leaves that are sometimes spotted with red. Pink, purple or white flowers are borne in conical clusters.

P. paniculata (garden phlox, summer phlox) are upright plants. The many cultivars vary in size and flower colour.

P. stolonifera (creeping phlox) is a low, spreading plant that bears flowers in several shades of purple.

P. subulata (moss phlox, moss pink) is very low growing and bears flowers in various colours. The foliage is evergreen.

Features: spring, summer or autumn flowers
Flower colour: white, blue, purple, orange, pink, red **Height:** 5 cm–1.2 m (2"–4') **Spread:** 30–90 cm (12–36") **Hardiness:** zones 2–8

Pinks

Dianthus

This genus contains a wide variety of plants, from tiny and delicate to large and robust. Many have spice-scented flowers.

Growing

Pinks prefer **full sun** but tolerate some light shade. A **well-drained, neutral or alkaline** soil is required. The most important factor is drainage—pinks hate to stand in water. Rocky outcroppings make up the native habitat of many species.

Tips

Pinks are excellent for rock gardens and rock walls, and for edging flower borders and walkways. They can also be used in cutting gardens and even as groundcovers. To prolong blooming, deadhead as the flowers fade, but leave a few flowers to go to seed.

Recommended

D. x allwoodii (allwood pinks) is a hybrid that forms a compact mound and bears flowers in a wide range of colours. Many cultivars are available.

D. deltoides (maiden pink) forms a mat of foliage and flowers in shades of red.

D. gratianopolitanus (cheddar pink) is long lived and forms a very dense mat of evergreen, silver grey foliage with sweet-scented flowers mostly in shades of pink.

D. plumarius (cottage pink) is noteworthy for its role in the development of many popular cultivars known collectively as garden pinks. The flowers can be single, semi-double or fully double and are available in many colours.

Features: sometimes-fragrant spring or summer flowers, attractive foliage **Flower colour:** pink, red, white, purple **Height:** 15–30 cm (6–12") **Spread:** 20–45 cm (8–18") **Hardiness:** zones 2–8

Sedum

Sedum

Some 300 to 500 species of sedum are distributed throughout the Northern Hemisphere. Many sedums are grown for their foliage, which can range in colour from steel grey-blue and green to red and burgundy.

Growing

Sedums prefer **full sun** but tolerate partial shade. The soil should be of **average fertility**, **very well drained** and **neutral to alkaline**. Divide in spring when needed.

Tips

Low-growing sedums make wonderful groundcovers and additions to rock gardens

or rock walls. They also edge beds and borders beautifully. Taller sedums give a lovely late-season display in a bed or border.

Recommended

S. acre (gold moss stonecrop) is a low-growing, wide-spreading plant that bears small, yellow-green flowers.

S. 'Autumn Joy' (autumn joy sedum) is a popular upright hybrid. The flowers open pink or red and later fade to deep bronze.

S. spectabile (showy stonecrop) is an upright species with pink flowers. Cultivars are available.

S. spurium (two-row stonecrop) forms a low, wide mat of foliage with deep pink or white flowers. Many cultivars are available and are often grown for their colourful foliage.

Also called: stonecrop **Features:** summer to autumn flowers, decorative fleshy foliage **Flower colour:** yellow, white, red or pink; plant also grown for foliage **Height:** 5–60 cm (2–24") **Spread:** 30–60 cm (12–24") or more **Hardiness:** zones 2–8

Snowdrop Anemone

Anemone

There is nothing quite so pretty as a clump of anemone growing in a shade garden in early spring. Anemone blossoms sparkle in the sunshine while the wind gently moves each petal for all to see.

Growing

Anemones grow well in **sun** or **partial shade** in **humus-rich, moist, well-drained** soil. Divide in early spring or late fall, and grow them in containers for a year before planting them back in the garden in spring.

Tips

Anemones make beautiful additions to lightly shaded borders, woodland gardens and rock gardens. They look magnificent planted en masse.

Recommended

A. sylvestris (snowdrop anemone) does well in woodland settings. Its late-spring flowers are white with yellow centres and are single in form. The tall, wiry flower stems emerge through lacy, ornate, bushy foliage.

Several cultivars are available. 'Grandiflora' bears large, nodding blossoms and 'Elisa Fellmann' produces semi-double flowers.

Also called: windflower **Features:** attractive flowers and foliage **Flower colour:** pink, red, purple, blue, yellow, white **Height:** 30–60 cm (12–24") **Spread:** 30–60 cm (12–24") **Hardiness:** zones 2–8

Speedwell

Veronica

at-forming species of speedwell wind their way around the stalks of other plants and do their part to suppress weeds, while the taller speedwells punctuate the front or middle of the bed with their spikes of white, pink or violet flowers.

Growing

Speedwells prefer **full sun** but tolerate partial shade. The soil should be of **average fertility, moist** and **well drained**. Once established, speedwells tolerate short periods of drought. Lack of sun and excessive moisture and nitrogen may be partly to blame for the sloppy habits of some speedwells. Frequent dividing ensures strong, vigorous growth and decreases the chances of flopping. Divide in autumn or spring every two or three years.

When the flowers begin to fade, remove the entire spike where it joins the plant to encourage rapid reblooming. For tidy plants, shear back to 15 cm (6") in June.

Tips

Prostrate speedwell is useful in a rock garden or at the front of a perennial border. Spike speedwell works well in masses in a bed or border.

Recommended

V. prostrata (prostrate speedwell) is a low-growing, spreading plant with blue or occasionally pink flowers. Many cultivars are available. (Zones 3–8)

V. spicata (spike speedwell) is a low, mounding plant with stems that flop over when they get too tall. It bears spikes of blue flowers. Many cultivars of different flower colours are available. (Zones 2–8)

This plant's genus name honours St. Veronica, who is said to have wiped the brow of Jesus on his way to Calvary.

Also called: Veronica **Features:** summer flowers, varied habits **Flower colour:** white, pink, purple, blue **Height:** 15–90 cm (6–36") **Spread:** 30–60 cm (12–24") **Hardiness:** zones 2–8

Amur Maackia
Maackia

Amur maackia comes from a lesser-known group of trees, but it deserves a place in the prairie landscape. Its smaller stature, elegant form, tough disposition and uniquely shaped, sweetly fragrant flowers could make it an Alberta standard.

Growing

Amur maackia grows best in **full sun**. It will adapt to most soil conditions but prefers **poor, acidic** or **alkaline** soils with **adequate drainage**.

Tips

Amur maackia works well as a specimen tree where it can show off its physical attributes, such as in a smaller-sized front yard. This tree is small enough to provide a little shade on a deck or patio without overtaking an entire yard.

Recommended

M. amurensis is a small tree that bears creamy white flower spikes on top of the branch tips that reach to the sky. The branching and overall form is rather flat but stunning. Small pea-like pods follow after the flowers fall.

Amur maackia is considered to be a clean tree with a neat habit, tolerant of poor conditions and requiring little care.

This tree is capable of fixing atmospheric nitrogen, which enables it to convert nitrogen gas into available nitrogen compounds.

Features: form, flowers, foliage
Habit: spreading, small deciduous tree
Flower colour: pale yellow to creamy white **Height:** 6–9 m (20–30')
Spread: 6–8 m (20–25')
Hardiness: zones 3–7

Ash

Fraxinus

The ash is not flashy, but it has many solid qualities. Its fall colours are gently glowing and luminous, a harmonious complement to the vivid oranges and reds of other autumn showoffs.

Growing

Ash grows best in **full sun**. The soil should be **fertile** and **moist** with lots of room for root growth. These trees will tolerate drought, poor soil, salt and pollution.

Tips

Ash is a quick-growing shade tree. It grows well in the moist soil alongside streams and ponds or in low-lying areas that never seem to dry out.

Recommended

F. mandshurica (Manchurian ash) is more compact in form, seedless and very hardy.

F. nigra (black ash, swamp ash) grows very tall and wide. Seedless cultivars are available, and offer great fall colour and longer periods in leaf.

F. pennsylvanica (green ash, red ash) is an irregular, spreading, seedless tree. It grows very tall and equally as wide. Its foliage turns yellow, sometimes with orange or red, in fall.

Features: fall colour, fast growth, habit
Habit: upright or spreading, deciduous tree
Height: 15–24 m (50–80') **Spread:** 7.5–24 m (25–80') **Hardiness:** zones 3–8

Aspen
Populus

When you mention aspen or poplar, the response is often a scowl based on a general dislike for the larger aspen varieties of old. The most popular varieties available today are vastly different from their cousins, which were considered messy and a nuisance.

Growing
Aspens prefer to grow in **full sun**. They are adaptable to any type of soil but prefer **deep soil** that is **rich**, **moist** and **well drained**.

Tips
The most common aspens of late are the columnar varieties. Perfect for narrow or small spaces and for use as privacy screens, these clean, vigorous trees can be left as single specimens or planted in rows or groups for impact.

Recommended
P. x *canescens* 'Tower' (tower poplar) closely resembles the more popular Swedish columnar aspen in appearance but is both wider and taller with a slightly more aggressive root system.

P. tremula 'Erecta' (Swedish columnar aspen) has rounded leaves that 'tremble' in the slightest breeze. This seedless cultivar has a columnar growth habit and is very popular because of its shallow and non-invasive root system, vigorous growth and overall form. Its narrow habit makes it popular for privacy screening in newer housing developments where there's little space to waste or time to wait for growth.

Columnar trees can lend a formal touch to a flat landscape.

Also called: poplar **Features:** foliage; form; growth rate; long, greenish catkins **Habit:** oval, columnar, deciduous trees **Height:** 9–21 m (30–70') **Spread:** 1.5–3 m (5–10') **Hardiness:** zones 1–7

Barberry

Berberis

The variations available in plant size, foliage colour and fruit make barberry a real workhorse of the plant world.

Growing

Barberry develops the best fall colour when grown in **full sun**, but it tolerates partial shade. Any **well-drained** soil is suitable. This plant tolerates drought and urban conditions but suffers in poorly drained, wet soil.

Tips

Large barberry plants make great hedges with formidable prickles. Barberry can also be included in shrub and mixed borders. Small cultivars can be grown in rock gardens, in raised beds and along rock walls.

Recommended

B. thunbergii (Japanese barberry) is a dense shrub with a broad, rounded habit. The foliage is bright green and turns variable shades of orange, red or purple in fall. Yellow spring flowers are followed by glossy red fruit later in summer. Many cultivars have been developed for their variable foliage colour, including shades of purple, yellow and variegated varieties.

Extracts from the rhizomes of Berberis have been used to treat rheumatic fever and other inflammatory disorders.

Features: foliage, flowers, fruit **Habit:** prickly deciduous shrub **Height:** 30 cm–1.5 m (12"–5')
Spread: 40 cm–1.5 m (18"–5')
Hardiness: zones 4–8

Birch

Betula

$\mathcal{I}$t seems like birch trees have graced the prairie landscape forever. Although birch has struggled in times of drought, it has earned a respected status throughout the region.

Growing

Birches grow well in **full sun**, **partial shade** or **light shade**. The soil should be of **average to rich fertility**, **well drained** and **moist**. Many birch species naturally grow in wet areas, such as alongside streams. They don't, however, like permanently soggy conditions. Prune only in late summer or fall to prevent sap loss.

Tips

Often used as a specimen tree, a birch's small leaves and open canopy provide light shade that allows perennials, annuals or lawns to flourish beneath.

Recommended

B. papyrifera (paper birch, white birch) is native to parts of Alberta and is a staple in many residential settings. It has creamy white bark that peels off in layers, exposing cinnamon-coloured bark beneath. Yellowish catkins dangle from the branches in early spring. Cultivars with purple leaves or columnar forms are also available.

B. pendula (weeping birch, European birch) has brown, papery bark that turns white with maturity. Cultivars that offer lacy leaves, smaller forms or weeping or columnar growth habits are also available.

Rough-textured, black, diamond-shaped patterns are commonly found on the bark of older trees.

Features: foliage, habit, bark, winter and early-spring catkins **Habit:** open, deciduous tree **Height:** 9–15 m (30–50') **Spread:** 6–9 m (20–30') **Hardiness:** zones 2–8

Caragana
Caragana

This plant is hardy to Zone 2, holds its own on dry, exposed sites and has the ability to fix nitrogen in the soil. When all other shrubs have succumbed to wicked conditions, caragana still thrives.

Caraganas are almost impossible to kill. They have superior heat and drought tolerance but fail in locations that are too moist.

Growing
Caragana prefers **full sun**, but will tolerate partial or light shade. Soil of **average to high fertility** is preferred. This plant will adapt to just about any growing conditions and tolerates dry, exposed locations.

Tips
Caragana plants are grown as windbreaks and formal or informal hedges. Caragana can be included in borders, and weeping forms are often used as specimen plants.

Recommended
C. arborescens is a large, twiggy, thorny shrub with upright or arching branches. Yellow, pea-like flowers are borne in late spring, followed by seedpods that ripen to brown in summer and rattle when blown by the wind. Grafted standards that resemble leafy umbrellas are available in various sizes, with either rounded or needle-like leaves.

Also called: peashrub **Features:** late-spring flowers, foliage, habit **Habit:** prickly, grafted, weeping or upright, rounded shrub
Height: 1–6 m (3–20') **Spread:** 2.5–5.5 m (8–18') **Hardiness:** zones 2–7

Cedar

Thuja

Cedars are rot resistant, durable and long lived, earning quiet admiration from gardeners everywhere.

Growing

Cedars prefer **full sun**, but tolerate light to partial shade. The soil should be of **average fertility, moist** and **well drained**. These plants enjoy humidity and will perform best in a location with some shelter from wind, especially in winter, when the foliage can easily dry out and give the entire plant a rather brown, drab appearance.

Tips

Large varieties of cedar make excellent specimen trees, and smaller cultivars can be used in foundation plantings and shrub borders and as formal or informal hedges.

Recommended

T. occidentalis (eastern arborvitae, eastern white cedar) is a narrow, pyramidal tree with scale-like evergreen needles. There are dozens of cultivars available, including shrubby dwarf varieties, varieties with yellow foliage and smaller upright varieties. **'Brandon'** grows tall and upright, and is most resistant to winterburn. **'Danica'** is a dwarf variety that grows to the size of a basketball. **'Holmstrup'** is an upright variety, but short in stature. **'Little Giant'** forms a medium-sized globe. (Zones 2–7; cultivars may be less cold hardy)

Deer enjoy eating the foliage of eastern arborvitae. Consider using western arborvitae, which is relatively resistant to deer browsing, instead.

Also called: arborvitae **Features:** foliage, bark, form **Habit:** small to large, evergreen shrub or tree **Height:** 60 cm–15 m (2–50') **Spread:** 60 cm–6 m (2–20') **Hardiness:** zones 2–8

Cotoneaster
Cotoneaster

With their diverse sizes, shapes, flowers, fruit and foliage, cotoneasters are so versatile that they border on being overused.

Growing
Cotoneasters grow well in **full sun or partial shade**. The soil should be of **average fertility** and **well drained**.

Tips
Cotoneasters can be included in shrub or mixed borders. Low spreaders work well as groundcovers and shrubby species can be used to form hedges. Larger species are grown as small specimen trees and some low growers are grafted onto standards and grown as small, weeping trees.

Recommended
There are many cotoneasters to choose from: *C. acutifolius* (Peking cotoneaster) is the frequently used hedging form. *C. adpressus* (creeping cotoneaster) is a groundcover plant, as its name implies. *C. apiculatus* (cranberry cotoneaster) is an upright shrubby plant. *C.* x 'Hessei' (Hess cotoneaster) and *C. horizontalis* (rockspray cotoneaster) are other low-growing groundcover varieties. These are just a few possibilities; your local garden centre will be able to help you find a suitable one for your garden.

Although cotoneaster berries are not poisonous, they can cause stomach upset if eaten in large quantities. The foliage may be toxic.

Features: foliage, early-summer flowers, persistent fruit, variety of forms **Habit:** evergreen or deciduous groundcover, shrub or small tree **Height:** 30 cm–3 m (1–10') **Spread:** 1–2 m (3–7') **Hardiness:** zones 3–8

Currant

Ribes

Currant shrubs have proven highly useful to northern gardeners. Certain varieties are grown for their ornamental attributes while others produce mouthwatering fruit that can be eaten right off the bush or used to make jellies, jams and pies.

Growing

Currant grows well in **full sun** or **partial shade**. The soil should be of **average fertility, moist, well drained** and **rich in organic matter**.

Tips

Currant can be used in a shrub or mixed border, on the edge of a garden bed or as a hedge. Alpine currant makes an excellent hedge.

Recommended

R. alpinum (alpine currant) is a dense, bushy, rounded shrub that tolerates shade and pollution. It bears yellow-green flowers in spring, followed by red berries on the female plants.

R. aureum (golden currant) is an upright shrub with slightly arching stems and blue-green foliage that turns red in fall. Fragrant, yellow flowers are borne in spring, followed by black berries.

R. silvestre (red currant) is an open shrub that produces clusters of yellow-green flowers in spring, followed by translucent, early-ripening, red fruit.

Currants and gooseberries are closely related. In general, gooseberries are spinier than currants.

Features: spring flowers, fruit, foliage **Habit:** upright, deciduous shrub with arching stems **Height:** 1–2.5 m (3–8') **Spread:** 1–2.5 m (3–8') **Hardiness:** zones 2–7

Dogwood
Cornus

Growing

Dogwoods grow equally well in **full sun, light shade** or **partial shade**, with a slight preference for light shade. The soil should be of **average to high fertility, high in organic matter, neutral or slightly acidic** and **well drained**.

Tips

Use shrub dogwoods along the edge of a woodland garden, in a shrub or mixed border, alongside a house or near a pond, water feature or patio. They look better in groups than left as single specimens.

Recommended

C. alba (red-twig dogwood, Tartarian dogwood) and *C. sericea* (*C. stolonifera*, red-osier dogwood) are grown for their bright red stems, which provide winter interest. Cultivars are available with stems in varied shades of red, orange and yellow. Fall foliage often turns an attractive colour. (Zones 2–8)

C. alternifolia (pagoda dogwood) can be grown as a large, multi-stemmed shrub or a small, single-stemmed tree. The branches have an attractive, layered appearance. Clusters of small white flowers appear in early summer. (Zones 3–8)

C. racemosa (grey dogwood) is a widespreading shrub with grey stems and clusters of white fruit on red stems. The foliage turns a warm shade of purple in the fall. (Zones 3-8)

Whether your garden is wet, dry, sunny or shaded, there is a dogwood for almost every condition. Stem colour, leaf variegation, fall colour, growth habit, soil adaptability and hardiness are all positive attributes to be found in the dogwoods.

Features: late-spring to early-summer flowers, fall foliage, stem colour, fruit, habit **Habit:** deciduous, large shrubs or small trees **Height:** 1.5–4.5 m (5–15') **Spread:** 1.5–6 m (5–20') **Hardiness:** zones 2–8

Elder
Sambucus

Elders work well in a naturalized garden. Cultivars are available that will provide light texture in a dark area, dark foliage in a bright area or variegated yellow leaves and colourful stems in brilliant sunshine.

Growing

Elders grow well in **full sun or partial shade**. Cultivars and varieties grown for interesting leaf colour develop the best colour in light or partial shade. The soil should be of **average fertility, moist** and **well drained**. These plants tolerate dry soil once established.

Tips

Elders can be used in a shrub or mixed border, in a natural woodland garden or next to a pond or other water feature.

Varieties with interesting or colourful foliage can be used as specimen plants or focal points in the garden.

Recommended

S. canadensis (American elder/elderberry), *S. nigra* (European elder/elderberry, black elder/elderberry) and *S. racemosa* (European red elder/elderberry) are rounded shrubs with white or pinkish white flowers followed by red or dark purple berries. Cultivars are available with green, yellow, bronze or purple foliage and deeply divided feathery foliage.

Also called: elderberry **Features:** early-summer flowers, fruit, foliage **Habit:** large, bushy, deciduous shrub **Height:** 1.5–3 m (5–10') **Spread:** 1.5–3 m (5–10') **Hardiness:** zones 2–8

Elm
Ulmus

Edmonton has the largest concentration of uninfected American elms in the province, with over 65,000 specimens valued at more than $210 million. Dutch elm disease (DED) has reduced the presence of elms dramatically but the introduction of resistant species and cultivars should encourage their use once again.

Growing

Elms grow well in **full sun** or **partial shade**. They adapt to most soil conditions but prefer a **moist, fertile soil**. Prune out all dead wood that provides beetle habitat. Prune live wood only during the winter.

Tips

Smaller species and cultivars make attractive specimen and shade trees, while larger trees look attractive on larger properties and in parks, where they have plenty of room to grow.

Recommended

U. americana (American elm) is a vase-shaped tree with arching branches. It grows very tall and wide. Consider cultivars that resist Dutch elm disease, such as the Alberta-bred **'Brandon'** elm.

DED is a realistic threat, but it can be prevented if people know what to look for. Learn everything you can about DED to protect our elms.

Features: vase-shaped growth habit, form, fall colour **Habit:** vase-shaped, open, deciduous tree **Flower colour:** inconspicuous **Height:** 17–34 m (55–110') **Spread:** 11–18 m (35–60') **Hardiness:** zones 2–8

Euonymus
Euonymus

Burning bush makes a fine specimen and works well as a background or border plant for stunning fall colour and interesting bark. The wintercreeper euonymus, with its interesting leaf colourings and plant habits, also has many uses.

Growing
Euonymus species prefer **full sun** and tolerate light or partial shade. Soil of **average to rich fertility** is preferable, but any **moist, well-drained** soil will do.

Tips
E. alatus can be grown in a shrub or mixed border, as a specimen, in a naturalistic garden or as a hedge. Dwarf cultivars can be used to create informal hedges. *E. fortunei* can be grown as a shrub in borders or as a hedge. It is an excellent substitute for the more demanding boxwood. The trailing habit also makes it useful as a groundcover or climber.

Recommended
E. alatus (burning bush, winged euonymus) is an attractive, open, mounding, deciduous shrub with vivid red fall foliage. Winter interest is provided by the corky ridges, or wings, that grow on the stems and branches. Cultivars are available. (Zones 3-8)

E. fortunei (wintercreeper euonymus) as a species is rarely grown owing to the wide and attractive variety of cultivars. These can be prostrate, climbing or mounding evergreens, often with attractive, variegated foliage. Winter protection is necessary. (Zones 4-8)

E. nana turkestanica (Turkestan burning bush) is a sprawling shrub with a rounded, upright habit. It produces fine-textured foliage and showy pink pendent flowers. Good fall colour. (Zones 2-8)

Features: foliage, corky stems (*E. alatus*), habit **Habit:** deciduous and evergreen shrub, small tree, groundcover or climber **Height:** 30 cm–2 m (12"–6') **Spread:** 60 cm–2 m (24"–6') **Hardiness:** zones 2–8

False Cypress
Chamaecyparis

The oils in the foliage of false cypresses may be irritating to sensitive skin.

Conifer shoppers are blessed with a marvelous selection of false cypresses that offers colour, size, shape and growth habits not available in most other evergreens.

Growing
False cypresses prefer **full sun**. The soil should be **fertile, moist, neutral to acidic** and **well drained**. Alkaline soils are tolerated. In shaded areas, growth may be sparse or thin.

Tips
Tree varieties are used as specimen plants. The dwarf and slow-growing cultivars are used in borders and rock gardens and as bonsai. False cypress shrubs can be grown near the house or as evergreen specimens in large containers.

Recommended
There are several available species of false cypress and many cultivars. The scaley foliage can come in a drooping or strand form, in fan-like or feathery sprays. It may be dark green, bright green or yellow. Plant forms vary too, from mounding or rounded to tall and pyramidal or narrow with pendulous branches. Check with your local garden centre or nursery to see what is available.

Features: foliage, habit, cones **Habit:** narrow, pyramidal, evergreen tree or shrub
Height: 50 cm–9 m (18"–30') **Spread:** 1.2–5 m (4–16') **Hardiness:** zones 4–8

Fir

Abies

Many people aren't aware that there are a number of hardy and beautiful fir varieties available that will thrive on the prairies. The trees are stately in appearance and the compact shrub varieties are ideal for rock gardens and small yards.

Growing

Firs usually prefer **full sun** but tolerate partial shade. The soil should be **rich, moist, neutral to acidic** and **well drained**. Firs prefer a **sheltered** site out of the wind, and they generally will not tolerate polluted city conditions. *A. concolor* tolerates pollution, heat and drought better than other *Abies* species.

Tips

Firs make impressive specimen trees in large areas. Dwarf cultivars can be included in shrub borders or planted as specimens.

Recommended

A. balsamea (balsam fir) looks pyramidal when it's young but narrows as it ages. (Zones 3–6)

A. concolor (white fir) is a large, pyramidal to conic tree. The needles have a whitish coating, which gives the tree a hazy blue appearance. Cultivars with even whiter needles are also available. (Zones 3–7)

A. lasiocarpa (subalpine fir) is a narrow, pyramidal tree that grows large in moist, sheltered locations. (Zones 3–8)

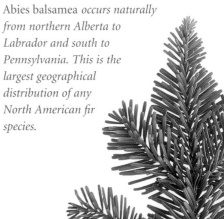

Abies balsamea *occurs naturally from northern Alberta to Labrador and south to Pennsylvania. This is the largest geographical distribution of any North American fir species.*

Features: foliage, cones **Habit:** narrow, pyramidal or columnar, evergreen tree **Height:** 50 cm–21 m (24"–70') **Spread:** 1–8 m (3–25') **Hardiness:** zones 3–7

Flowering Cherry, Plum & Almond
Prunus

Cherries and plums are so beautiful and uplifting after the grey days of winter that few gardeners can resist them.

Growing

These flowering fruit trees prefer **full sun**. The soil should be of **average fertility, moist** and **well drained**. Shallow roots will emerge from the lawn if the tree is not getting sufficient water.

Tips

Tree and shrub species are beautiful as specimen plants and many are small enough for most gardens. Small species and cultivars can be included in borders or grouped to form informal hedges or barriers. Double-flowering plum, nanking cherry and purpleleaf sand cherry can be trained into informal hedges.

Recommended

A great number of *Prunus* varieties are popular throughout Alberta. *P. besseyi* (western sand cherry) is frequently used as a shrubby pollinator for plums. It bears glossy green foliage and white flowers. *P. x cistena* (purpleleaf sand cherry) is a shrub grown for its purple foliage and light pink flowers. *P. fruticosa* (Mongolian cherry) bears tasty sour cherries ideal for preserves and pies. *P. padus* (Mayday) bears pink or white blossoms in early spring. *P. mackii* (amur cherry) is a small, rounded tree with attractive bark. *P. pennsylvanica* (pin cherry) produces sour cherries on a slender, often shrubby tree. *P. tomentosa* (nanking cherry) is a rounded, blooming shrub with tart red berries. *P. virginiana* (chokecherry) is a medium-sized tree with dark burgundy foliage, tiny white flowers and fruit adored by birds.

Also called: Mayday, chokecherry
Features: spring to early-summer flowers, fruit, bark, fall foliage **Habit:** upright, rounded, spreading or weeping, deciduous tree or shrub
Height: 1–10.5 m (3–35') **Spread:** 1–9 m (3–30') **Hardiness:** zones 2–8

Forsythia
Forsythia

Forsythia's bright, lemon yellow flowers are indicators of warmer days ahead. While other plants have yet to wake from their deep winter sleep, forsythia blooms like crazy. Copious numbers of leaves follow the flowers throughout the warm summer months.

Growing

Forsythias grow best in **full sun** but tolerate light shade. The soil should be of **average fertility**, **moist** and **well drained**.

Tips

These shrubs look gorgeous in flower. Plant one in a shrub or mixed border where other flowering plants can take over once the forsythia's early blooming season has passed.

Recommended

F. x *intermedia* (border forsythia) is a large shrub with upright stems that arch as they mature. Yellow flowers emerge before the leaves in early to mid-spring. Many cultivars have been developed from this hybrid.

F. ovata (early forsythia) is an upright, spreading shrub that bears bright yellow, pendant flowers in early spring, followed by dense tufts of smooth foliage. A number of cultivars are available.

Correct pruning after flowering is finished will keep forsythias looking attractive. Flowers are produced on growth that is usually at least two years old. On mature plants, cut one-third of the oldest growth back to the ground each year.

Features: early-spring blooming, dense growth habit **Habit:** deciduous, upright, bushy
Flower colour: yellow **Height:** 1.8 m (6')
Spread: 1.8 m (6') **Hardiness:** zones 3–8

Hackberry
Celtis

Although hackberry isn't a top-ten seller in the prairies yet, it should be. It tolerates any and all conditions in Alberta, and responds with brawn and grace.

Growing
Hackberry prefers **full sun**. It adapts to a variety of soil types including poor and dry soils. **Deep soils** with **adequate moisture** and **drainage** are best.

Tips
Hackberry is an ideal shade tree specimen for expansive, windy areas. It grows as tall as it does wide, and requires lots of space to reach its full size without conflict.

Recommended
C. occidentalis is a medium to large tree with a rounded head. The head is made up of arching branches covered in simple but classic foliage. Inconspicuous flowers emerge in spring followed by dark red or purple pea-sized fruits in fall.

Hackberry has everything to offer but asks little in return. It will provide magnificent foliar colour in the fall and cool shade in the hot summer months.

Also called: American hackberry, common hackberry **Features:** form, hardiness, colourful berries, tolerance to poor conditions
Habit: high-headed, oval, deciduous tree
Flower colour: inconspicuous **Height:** 9–15 m (30–50') **Spread:** 9–15 m (30–50')
Hardiness: zones 2–8

Hawthorn

Crataegus

Hawthorns are uncommonly beautiful trees that offer a generous spring show of beautiful, miniature rose-like blossoms, persistent glossy red fruit and good fall colour.

Growing

Hawthorns grow equally well in **full sun or partial shade**. They adapt to any **well-drained** soil and tolerate urban conditions.

Tips

Hawthorns can be grown as specimen plants for informal landscapes and gardens. They require little care and are the ideal flowering ornamentals for small spaces.

These trees are small enough to include in most gardens. With the stiff, 5 cm (2") long, sharp thorns, however, a hawthorn might not be a good selection if there are children about.

Recommended

C. crus-galli 'Inermis' (thornless cockspur hawthorn) is a small, drought-tolerant tree, bearing white flowers followed by red, persistent fruits and orange fall colour. (Zones 4–8)

C. laevigata (*C. oxycantha*; English hawthorn) is a low-branching, rounded tree with zigzag layers of thorny branches. It bears white or pink flowers, followed by red fruit in late summer. Many cultivars are available. (Zones 4–8)

C. x *mordensis* is a small ornamental tree with double white or pink flowers followed by sparse red berries. A few cultivars are available. (Zones 3–8)

Features: late-spring or early-summer flowers, fruit, foliage, thorny branches **Habit:** rounded, deciduous trees, often with a zigzagged, layered branch pattern and twisted trunk **Height:** 4.5–9 m (15–30') **Spread:** 3–6 m (10–20') **Hardiness:** zones 3–8

Honeysuckle

Lonicera

Honeysuckle produces beautiful, exotic flowers on both its shrub and vine varieties. It's easy to care for and offers a little tropical flare in late spring.

A wide variety of different species and cultivars are available in smaller, compact forms, different flower colours and varied foliage.

Growing

Honeysuckles grow well in **full sun** and **partial shade**. The soil should be **average to fertile** and **well drained**. Climbing honeysuckles prefer a **moist, humus-rich soil**.

Tips

Shrubby honeysuckles can be used in mixed borders, in naturalized gardens and as hedges. Most are large and take up a lot of space when mature. A climbing honeysuckle can be trained to grow up a trellis, fence, arbour or other structure.

Recommended

L. tatarica (tatarian honeysuckle) is a large, bushy, deciduous shrub that grows very tall with an equal spread. It bears pink, white or red flowers in late spring and early summer.

Features: flowers, habit, fruit **Habit:** rounded, upright shrub or twining climber **Height:** 3–4 m (10–12') **Spread:** 3 m (10') **Hardiness:** zones 3–8

Hydrangea

Hydrangea

Hydrangeas have many attractive qualities, including showy, often long-lasting flowers and glossy green leaves, some of which turn beautiful colours in fall.

Growing

Hydrangeas grow well in **full sun or partial shade,** and some species tolerate full shade. Shade or partial shade will reduce leaf and flower scorch in hotter gardens. The soil should be of **average to high fertility, humus rich, moist** and **well drained.** These plants perform best in cool, moist conditions.

Tips

Hydrangeas come in many forms and have many uses in the landscape. They can be included in shrub or mixed borders, used as specimens or informal barriers and planted in groups or containers.

Recommended

H. arborescens (smooth hydrangea) is a rounded shrub that flowers well even in shady conditions. This species is rarely grown in favour of the cultivars that bear large clusters of showy white blossoms.

H. macrophylla (bigleaf hydrangea) is a large-flowered species that repeat blooms almost all summer long. The blooms are often pink in alkaline soils and display a blue cast in acidic soil. Newer cultivars are now available in a variety of colours and more than a few are hardy to zone 4.

H. paniculata (panicle hydrangea) is a spreading to upright large shrub or small tree that bears white flowers from late summer to early fall. **'Grandiflora'** (peegee hydrangea) is a commonly available cultivar.

Features: flowers, habit, foliage, bark
Habit: deciduous; mounding or spreading shrubs or trees **Height:** 1 m (3')
Spread: 1 m (3') **Hardiness:** zones 3–8

Juniper
Juniperus

With the wide variety of junipers available, from low creeping plants to upright pyramidal forms, there are endless uses for them in the garden.

Growing
Junipers prefer **full sun** but tolerate light shade. Ideally the soil should be of **average fertility** and **well drained**, but these plants tolerate most conditions.

Tips
Junipers can make prickly barriers and hedges, and they can be used in borders, as specimens or in groups. The larger species can be used to form windbreaks, while the low-growing species can be used in rock gardens and as groundcovers.

Recommended
Junipers vary from species to species and often within a species. Cultivars are available for all species and may differ significantly from the species. *J. chinensis* (Chinese juniper) is a conical tree or spreading shrub. *J. communis* (common juniper) is a low-growing, spreading species. *J. horizontalis* (creeping juniper) is a prostrate, creeping groundcover. *J. procumbens* (Japanese garden juniper) is a wide-spreading, stiff-branched, low shrub. *J. sabina* (savin juniper) is a low-growing, groundcover species. *J. scopulorum* (Rocky Mountain juniper) can be upright, rounded, weeping or spreading in form. *J. squamata* (single-seed juniper) forms a prostrate or low, spreading shrub or a small, upright tree. *J. virginiana* (eastern redcedar) is a durable tree, upright or wide spreading.

Wear long sleeves and gloves when handling junipers— the prickly foliage gives some gardeners a rash. Juniper 'berries' are poisonous if eaten in large quantities.

Features: foliage, variety of colour, size and habit **Habit:** conical or columnar tree, rounded or spreading shrub, prostrate groundcover; evergreen **Height:** 10 cm–4.8 m (4"–16') **Spread:** 60 cm–2.5 m (24"–8') **Hardiness:** zones 2–8

Kinnikinnick

Arctostaphylos

Kinnikinnick is a tough, hardy, shrubby groundcover with woody stems and smallish, leathery leaves. Its adorable flowers are followed by brightly coloured berries and striking fall hues.

Growing

Kinnikinnick grows well in **full sun** or **partial shade**. The soil should be of **poor to average fertility**, **acidic** and **moist**. Kinnikinnick will adapt to alkaline soil.

Tips

Kinnikinnick can be used as a groundcover or can be included in a rock garden. It can be slow to get started, but once established, it is a vigorous, wide-spreading grower.

Recommended

A. uva-ursi is a shrub with pinkish white flowers that appear in late spring, followed by berries that ripen to bright red. The cultivars have similar white flowers and red fruit, but their leaves turn bright red in winter.

With its lustrous, dark green foliage and red fruit in summer, kinnikinnick is one of the prettiest groundcovers.

Also called: bearberry **Features:** late-spring flowers, fruit, foliage **Habit:** low-growing, mat-forming, evergreen shrub **Flower colour:** pinkish white **Height:** 10–15 cm (4–6") **Spread:** 50 cm–1.2 m (18"–4') **Hardiness:** zones 2–7

Larch

Larix

The larch makes an interesting specimen tree. It is one of the few needled trees that loses its foliage each year.

Growing
Larch grows best in **full sun**. The soil should be of **average fertility**, **acidic**, **moist** and **well drained**. Though tolerant of most conditions, this tree doesn't like dry or chalky soils.

Tips
This deciduous conifer likes cool, wet sites. It detests heat and drought, so careful placement is necessary.

Recommended
L. decidua (European larch) is a large, narrow, pyramidal tree with soft, green needles that turn bronzy yellow in the fall. A weeping cultivar and a tall, conical variety exist as well.

L. laricina (tamarack, Eastern larch) is an open, pyramidal tree with drooping branchlets. It grows very tall and narrow, and is tolerant of wet locations. This native larch turns a rich, burnished gold in fall before losing its needles.

The size of the low, weeping cultivars suit most residential gardens.

Features: summer and fall foliage, habit
Habit: pyramidal, deciduous conifer
Height: 3–24 m (10–80') **Spread:** 3–9 m (10–30') **Hardiness:** zones 1–7

Lilac
Syringa

There is no end to the colours, sizes, shapes and scents of lilacs available. An Alberta garden would feel incomplete without at least one lilac.

Growing

Lilacs grow best in **full sun**. The soil should be **fertile, humus rich** and **well drained**. These plants tolerate open, windy locations.

Tips

Include lilacs in a shrub or mixed border or use them to create an informal hedge. Japanese tree lilac can be used as a specimen tree.

Recommended

S. x *hyacinthiflora* (hyacinth-flowered lilac, early-flowering lilac) are hardy, upright hybrids that become spreading as they mature. Clusters of fragrant flowers appear two weeks earlier than French lilacs. The leaves turn reddish purple in fall. (Zones 3–7)

S. meyeri (Meyer lilac) is a compact, rounded shrub that bears fragrant pink or lavender flowers. (Zones 3–7)

S. patula (Manchurian lilac) is an upright, vigorous shrub that offers cultivars in compact forms. (Zones 3–8)

S. prestoniae (Preston lilac) is an extremely hardy, dense, mounding shrub with crinkly foliage. It blooms approximately two weeks later than French lilacs. (Zones 2–8)

S. reticulata (Japanese tree lilac) is a small tree that bears white flowers. '**Ivory Silk**' has a more compact habit and produces more flowers than the species. (Zones 3–7)

S. vulgaris (French lilac, common lilac) is the shrub most people think of when they think of lilacs. It is a suckering, spreading shrub with an irregular habit that bears fragrant, lilac-coloured flowers. (Zones 3–8)

Features: late-spring to mid-summer flowers, habit
Flower colour: white, shades of pink and purple
Habit: rounded, deciduous shrub or small tree
Height: 1.2–7.5 m (4–25') **Spread:** 1.2–6 m (4–20')
Hardiness: zones 2–8

Linden
Tilia

In ancient folklore, linden flowers were thought to cure epilepsy. Linden is still used for various medicinal purposes today.

Lindens are picturesque shade trees with a signature gumdrop shape and sweet-scented flowers that capture the essence of summer.

Growing
Lindens grow best in **full sun**. The soil should be **average to fertile, moist** and **well drained**. These trees adapt to most pH levels but prefer an alkaline soil. They tolerate pollution and urban conditions.

Tips
Lindens are useful and attractive street trees, shade trees and specimen trees. Their tolerance of pollution and their moderate size make them ideal for city gardens.

Recommended
T. cordata (littleleaf linden) is a dense, pyramidal tree that may become rounded with age. It bears small, fragrant flowers with narrow, yellow-green bracts. Cultivars are available.

T. flavescens 'Dropmore' is an upright, pyramidal tree with a dense and compact crown. It bears pale yellow blooms in summer.

T. mongolica (Mongolian linden) is an upright, round-headed tree with exfoliating bark and spectacular fall colour. Cultivars are available.

Features: habit, foliage **Habit:** dense, pyramidal to rounded, deciduous tree **Height:** 9–13.5 m (30–45') **Spread:** 6–10.5 m (20–35') **Hardiness:** zones 3–8

Maple

Acer

Maples look attractive all year, with impressive foliage and hanging samaras in summer, vibrant leaf colour in fall and interesting bark and branch structure in winter.

Growing

Generally, maples do well in **full sun** or **light shade,** though this varies from species to species. The soil should be **fertile, moist, high in organic matter** and **well drained.**

Tips

Maples can be used as specimen trees, as large elements in shrub or mixed borders or as hedges. Some are useful as understorey plants bordering wooded areas; others can be grown in containers on patios or terraces. Most Japanese gardens showcase attractive smaller maples. Almost all maples can be used to create bonsai specimens.

Recommended

Maples are some of the most popular choices for shade or street trees. Many are very large when fully mature, but a few smaller species are useful in smaller gardens. Check with your local nursery or garden centre for availability and how to protect patio specimens throughout winter.

Maple fruits, called samaras, have wings that act like miniature helicopter rotors and help in seed dispersal.

Features: foliage, bark, winged fruit, fall colour, form, flowers **Habit:** small, multi-stemmed, deciduous tree or large shrub **Height:** 1.2–18 m (4–60') **Spread:** 1.2–14 m (4–45') **Hardiness:** zones 2–8

Mock-Orange
Philadelphus

Grow a mock-orange if only for its heavenly fragrance, which is reminiscent of orange blossoms.

Growing

Mock-oranges grow well in **full sun**, **partial shade** or **light shade**. The soil should be of **average fertility**, **humus rich**, **moist** and **well drained**.

Purchase some cultivars by name and description, or use your nose to select unknown plants.

Tips

Include mock-oranges in shrub or mixed borders. Use them in groups to create barriers and screens.

Recommended

P. coronarius (sweet mock-orange) is an upright, broadly rounded shrub with fragrant, white flowers. It grows quite tall and wide. Cultivars with variegated or chartreuse foliage are available.

P. lewisii is a smaller shrub with white, citrus-scented, single flowers that float atop dark green, contrasting foliage. A wide variety of cultivars that offer double flowers and differing heights and spreads are available.

Features: early-summer, fragrant, white flowers **Habit:** rounded, deciduous shrub with arching branches **Height:** 50 cm–3.5 m (18"–12') **Spread:** 50 cm–3.5 m (18"–12') **Hardiness:** zones 3–8

Mountain Ash

Sorbus

Mountain ash is grown for its attractive, oval form, spring display of white flowers and red, orange or yellow fall fruit that persists into winter. The berries provide important forage for birds and are a visual feast.

Growing

Mountain ash grows well in **full sun, partial shade** or **light shade**. Make sure it has **average to fertile, humus-rich, well-drained** soil.

Tips

Commonly grown as a specimen tree, mountain ash is also ideal in woodland and natural settings where it attracts a variety of wildlife to the garden.

Recommended

S. americana (American mountain ash) has an oval, low head and dark brown bark. Large clusters of fragrant, white flowers emerge in early spring followed by scarlet berries. Great fall colour.

S. aucuparia (European mountain ash) grows slightly taller than *S. americana* and bears large flower clusters followed by orange-red berries in fall. Some of the most popular columnar cultivars are related to this species.

S. decora (showy mountain ash) is much shorter and half the width of the more traditional varieties. *S. decora*'s blooming cycle exceeds that of its relatives, it is more resistant to fireblight and it displays magnificent fall colour.

Mountain ash varieties prefer to be planted on a higher elevation with excellent drainage to prevent rot.

Features: fall colour; white flowers; brightly coloured, persistent fruit **Habit:** rounded or oval, deciduous tree **Flower colour:** white **Height:** 5–12 m (16–40') **Spread:** 6.5–7.5 m (6–25') **Hardiness:** zones 2-7

Ninebark

Physocarpus

This attractive North American native deserves wider recognition, especially now that attractive cultivars, with foliage ranging in colour from yellow to purple, are available.

You may not actually find nine layers, but the peeling, flecked bark of ninebark does add interest to the winter landscape.

Growing

Ninebark grows well in **full sun or partial shade**. The best leaf colouring develops in a sunny location. The soil should be **fertile, acidic, moist** and **well drained**.

Tips

Ninebark can be included in a shrub or mixed border, in a woodland garden or in a wild garden.

Recommended

P. opulifolius (common ninebark) is a shrub with long, arching branches and exfoliating bark. It bears light pink or white flowers in early summer and fruit that ripens to reddish green or red in late fall. Several cultivars are available.

Also called: common ninebark
Features: early-summer flowers, fruit, bark, foliage **Habit:** upright, sometimes suckering, deciduous shrub **Height:** 1.5–2.5 m (5–8')
Spread: 1.5–2.5 m (5–8')
Hardiness: zones 2–8

Oak

Quercus

The oak's classic shape, outstanding fall colour, deep roots and long life are some of its many assets. Plant it for its individual beauty and for posterity.

Growing

Oaks grow well in **full sun** or **partial shade**. The soil should be **fertile, moist** and **well drained**. These trees can be difficult to establish; transplant them only when they are young.

Tips

Oaks are large trees that look best as specimens or planted in spacious yards and gardens and public spaces. Do not disturb the ground around the base of an oak; this tree is very sensitive to changes in grade.

Recommended

The following are a few popular oak species. *Q. alba* (white oak) is a rounded, spreading tree with peeling bark and purple-red fall colour. *Q. macrocarpa* (bur oak, mossycup oak) is a stately, medium-sized tree with an open and upright habit, an oval crown, very large and deeply lobed leaves and bark that is deeply textured and corky in appearance. *Q. palustris* (pin oak, swamp oak) is a strongly pyramidal tree with a slightly more vigorous growth habit than other species. *Q. rubra* (red oak) is a rounded, spreading tree with fall colour ranging from yellow to red-brown. A variety of cultivars are available for each species. Check with your local nursery or garden centre.

Features: summer and fall foliage, bark, habit, acorns **Habit:** large, rounded, spreading, deciduous tree **Height:** 15–25 m (50–80')
Spread: 7.5–15 m (25–50')
Hardiness: zones 3–8

Acorns are generally not edible. Those that are edible must usually be processed first to leach out the bitter tannins.

Ohio Buckeye

Aesculus

These trees give heavy shade, which is excellent for cooling buildings but can make it difficult to grow grass beneath them.

Ohio buckeye is a hardy specimen with admirable qualities ideal for the prairie landscape. Its relatives are equally as beautiful and deserving of more frequent use.

Growing

Ohio buckeye grow well in **full sun or partial shade**. The soil should be **fertile, moist** and **well drained**. These trees dislike excessive drought.

Tips

Ohio buckeye are used as specimen and shade trees. The roots can break up sidewalks and patios if planted too close together.

The smaller, shrubby horsechestnuts grow well near pond plantings and also make interesting specimens. Give them plenty of space as they can form large colonies.

Recommended

A. x *carnea* (horsechestnut) is a larger, low-headed globular tree with a dense canopy. It bears deeply lobed leaves and upright, showy, cone-shaped flowers in early summer. A number of cultivars that bear deep pink-red flowers are available. Check with your local garden centre to find what varieties are available.

A. glabra (Ohio buckeye) is an extremely hardy tree that produces masses of green-yellow flowers that emerge from each branch tip in early summer. The ornate foliage turns brilliant yellow in fall.

Features: early-summer flowers, foliage, spiny fruit **Habit:** rounded or spreading, deciduous tree or shrub **Height:** 7.5–10.5 m (25–35') **Spread:** 6–9 m (20–30') **Hardiness:** zones 3–8

Ornamental Crabapple

Malus

Pure white through deep pink flowers, heights between 1.5 and 7.5 m (5 and 25') with similar spreads, tolerance of winter's extreme cold and summer's baking heat, plus tiny fruit—from green to candy apple red—that persists through winter. What more could anyone ask from a tree?

Growing

Crabapples prefer **full sun** but tolerate partial shade. The soil should be of **average to rich fertility**, **moist** and **well drained**. These trees tolerate damp soil.

Many pests overwinter in the fruit, leaves or soil at the base of the tree. To prevent the spread of crabapple pests and diseases, clean up all the leaves and fruit that fall off the tree.

Tips

Crabapples make excellent specimen plants. Many varieties are quite small, so there is one to suit almost any size of garden. Crabapples' flexible young branches make them good choices for creating espalier specimens along a wall or fence.

Recommended

There are hundreds of ornamental crabapples available. When choosing a species, variety or cultivar, the most important attributes to look for are disease resistance and size at maturity. Ask for information about new, resistant cultivars at your local nursery or garden centre.

Features: spring flowers, late-season and winter fruit, fall foliage, habit, bark **Flower colour:** white, shades of pink **Habit:** rounded, mounded or spreading, small to medium, deciduous tree **Height:** 1.5–7.5 m (5–25') **Spread:** 1.8–6 m (6–20') **Hardiness:** zones 2–8

Pine

Pinus

Pines offer exciting possibilities for any garden. Exotic-looking pines are available with soft or stiff, silvery blue or grey needles; elegant, drooping branches; and flaky, copper-coloured bark.

Pine varieties generally thrive in our prairie climate. However, some pine species and cultivars are susceptible to both windburn and sunscald. Consult your local garden centre for recommendations.

Growing

Pines grow best in **full sun**. These trees adapt to most **well-drained** soils but do not tolerate polluted urban conditions.

Tips

Pines can be used as specimen trees, as hedges or to create windbreaks. Smaller cultivars can be included in shrub or mixed borders. These trees are not heavy feeders; fertilizing will encourage rapid new growth that is weak and susceptible to pest and disease problems.

Recommended

There are many available pines, both trees and shrubby dwarf plants. Check with your local garden centre or nursery to find out what is available.

Features: foliage, bark, cones, habit **Habit:** upright, columnar or spreading, evergreen trees **Height:** 90 cm–20 m (3–65') **Spread:** 90 cm–7.5 m (3–25') **Hardiness:** zones 2–8

Potentilla

Potentilla

Potentilla is a fuss-free shrub that blooms madly throughout summer.

Growing

Potentilla prefers **full sun** but tolerates partial or light shade. Preferably the soil should be of **poor to average fertility** and **well drained**. This plant tolerates most conditions, including sandy or clay soil and wet or dry conditions. Established plants are drought tolerant. Too much fertilizer or too rich a soil will encourage weak, floppy, disease-prone growth.

Tips

Potentilla is useful in a shrub or mixed border. The smaller cultivars can be included in rock gardens and on rock walls. On steep slopes, potentilla can prevent soil erosion and reduce time spent maintaining the lawn. It can even be used to form a low, informal hedge.

If your potentilla's flowers fade in direct sun or hot weather, move the plant to a cooler location with some shade from the hot afternoon sun. Colours should revive in fall as the weather cools. Plants with yellow flowers are least likely to be affected by heat and sun.

Recommended

Of the many cultivars of *P. fruticosa,* the following are a few of the most popular and interesting. '**Abbotswood**' is one of the best white-flowered cultivars. '**Pink Beauty**' bears pink, semi-double flowers. '**Tangerine**' has orange flowers and '**Yellow Gem**' has bright yellow flowers.

P. tridentata '**Nuuk**' (wineleaf potentilla) is a low-growing groundcover that bears tiny, white flowers in late spring. The small, green leaves change to fiery, reddish burgundy in fall.

Also called: shrubby cinquefoil
Features: flowers, foliage, habit
Habit: mounding, deciduous shrub
Height: 7 cm–1.2 m (3"–4') **Spread:** 30–90 cm (12–36") **Hardiness:** zones 2–8

Russian Cypress
Microbiota

Russian cypress is an extremely cold-hardy, shade-loving evergreen shrub that is finally getting the attention it deserves.

Growing

Russian cypress grows best in **partial to nearly full shade,** for it prefers life on the cool side, though it struggles in dense shade. It does well in full sun if mulched around the base and watered regularly. Soil should be of **moderate fertility** and must be **well drained** or the plant may die from root rot.

Tips

Russian cypress makes an excellent groundcover and can control erosion on slopes. It cascades gracefully down walls and raised planters and can be planted in shrub beds and rock gardens. It makes a good substitute for creeping juniper in a shady location.

Recommended

M. decussata is a wide-spreading evergreen shrub with creeping branches. Its flattened sprays of bright green foliage gradually darken over the summer. They turn an attractive reddish brown to bronze purple in the winter. The green colour returns very quickly in spring.

Don't be surprised when your entire Russian cypress turns a shade of plum in the fall.

Features: winter foliage, form **Habit:** evergreen, low-growing shrub **Height:** 30–45 cm (12–18")
Spread: 1.8–3 m (6–10') **Hardiness:** zones 2–8

Russian Olive

Elaeagnus

Russian olives are survivors. They can tough it out in dry conditions and even alongside highways, bombarded by exhaust and road salt. In a garden setting, they can be planted as transitional trees or used in difficult areas with poor-quality soil.

Growing

Russian olives grow best in **full sun**. Ideally, the soil should be a **well-drained**, **sandy loam** of **average to high fertility**. These plants adapt to poor soil because they can fix nitrogen from the air.

Tips

Russian olives are used in shrub or mixed borders, as hedges, screens and specimen plants. The fruits are edible but dry and mealy. The branches on some plants can be quite thorny.

Recommended

E. angustifolia is a rounded, spreading tree. The foliage often obscures the fragrant, yellow summer flowers and silvery yellow fruit. The main attractions of this species are its tolerance to adverse conditions and its narrow, silver grey leaves.

Features: fragrant summer flowers, summer foliage, fruit **Habit:** rounded, spreading, deciduous tree or shrub
Height: 4–6 m (12–20')
Spread: 4–6 m (12–20')
Hardiness: zones 2–8

Salt Bush

Halimodendron

Salt bush is a member of the pea family and bears sweet pea-like, lilac pink flowers. This tough, low-maintenance, drought-tolerant shrub is still uncommon but worth trying.

Growing

Salt bush prefers a **sunny, hot location**. The soil should be of **poor fertility** and **highly alkaline**. It thrives in the heat, on a sunny slope where excess moisture won't be a problem.

Tips

This spring bloomer can be trained to grow into a small tree form. It is also useful for privacy, wind or security screening or as an informal hedge.

Recommended

H. halodendron is a medium-sized shrub with downy, grey foliage on thorny stems. Pale lilac, lightly scented flowers emerge in early spring followed by long seedpods.

This shrub is perfect for gardens with poor soil and gardeners with little time.

Salt bush is another nitrogen-fixing plant, thanks to its legume family heritage.

Also called: salt tree **Features:** flowers, foliage, tolerance to drought, hardiness **Habit:** spreading, open, deciduous shrub or small tree **Flower colour:** lilac **Height:** 1.5–2 m (6–7') **Spread:** 1–1.5 m (3–5') **Hardiness:** zones 3–7

Serviceberry
Amelanchier

The *Amelanchier* species are first-rate North American natives, bearing lacy, white flowers in spring followed by edible berries. In fall, the foliage colour ranges from glowing apricot to deep red.

Growing

Serviceberries grow well in **full sun** or **light shade**. They prefer **acidic soil** that is **fertile, humus rich, moist** and **well drained**. They do adjust to drought.

Tips

With spring flowers, edible fruit, attractive leaves that turn red in fall and often artistic branch growth, serviceberries make beautiful specimen plants or even shade trees in small gardens. The shrubbier forms can be grown along the edges of a woodland or in a border. In the wild, these trees are often found growing near water sources, and are beautiful beside ponds or streams.

Recommended

Several popular species and hybrids are available. *A. arborea* (downy serviceberry, juneberry) is a small, single- or multi-stemmed tree; *A. canadensis* (shadblow serviceberry) is a large, upright, suckering shrub; *A.* x *grandiflora* (serviceberry) is a small, spreading, often multi-stemmed tree. All three have white flowers, purple fruit and good fall colour.

Serviceberry fruit can be used in place of blueberries in any recipe. They have a similar, but generally sweeter, flavour.

Also called: saskatoon, juneberry
Features: spring or early-summer flowers, edible fruit, fall colour, habit, bark **Habit:** single- or multi-stemmed, deciduous, large shrub or small tree **Height:** 4.5–7.5 m (15–25') **Spread:** 4.5–6 m (15–20') **Hardiness:** zones 3–8

Snowberry

Symphoricarpos

Snowberry is an excellent choice for naturalizing over large areas, and though its bloom is not spectacular, the bluish green foliage and white fruit are summer standouts.

Growing

Snowberry grows well in **full sun, partial or light shade**. This plant adapts to any soil that is **fertile** and **well drained**. It tolerates pollution, drought and exposure.

Tips

Snowberries can be used in shrub or mixed borders, as screens or informal hedges. They are great for use on hillsides, as their suckering roots bind the soil.

Recommended

S. albus is a rounded, suckering shrub with arching branches. The small, delicate, pinkish white summer flowers are rather inconspicuous but still attractive. The clusters of white berries that follow are interesting and persist through fall and early winter.

These low-maintenance shrubs spread readily and fill the gaps in shady areas.

Also called: coralberry **Features:** foliage, fall and winter fruit, habit **Habit:** rounded or spreading, deciduous shrub **Height:** 1–2 m (3–6') **Spread:** 1–2 m (3–6') **Hardiness:** zones 3–7

Spirea
Spiraea

Spireas, seen in so many gardens and with dozens of cultivars, remain undeniable favourites. With a wide range of forms, sizes and colours of both foliage and flowers, spireas have many possible uses in the landscape.

Growing

Spireas prefer **full sun**. To help prevent foliage burn, provide protection from very hot sun. The soil should be **fertile, acidic, moist** and **well drained**.

Tips

Spireas are used in shrub or mixed borders, in rock gardens and as informal screens and hedges.

Recommended

Two popular hybrid groups of the many species and cultivars follow. *S.* x *bumalda* (*S. japonica* 'Bumalda') is a low, broad, mounded shrub with pink flowers. It is rarely grown in favour of the many cultivars, which also have pink flowers, but with brightly coloured foliage. *S.* x *vanhouttei* (bridal wreath spirea, Vanhoutte spirea) is a dense, bushy shrub with arching branches and clusters of white flowers. Check at your local nursery or garden centre for additional varieties.

Features: summer flowers, habit **Habit:** round, bushy, deciduous shrub **Height:** 90 cm–2.4 m (3–8') **Spread:** 90 cm–2.4 m (3–8') **Hardiness:** zones 3–8

Spruce
Picea

Spruce tree and shrub specimens are some of the most commonly grown evergreens throughout the prairies. Grow spruce where they have enough room to spread then let them branch all the way to the ground.

Growing

Spruce trees grow best in **full sun**. The soil should be **deep, moist, well drained** and **neutral to acidic**. These trees generally don't like hot, dry or polluted conditions. Spruce are best grown from small, young stock as they dislike being transplanted when larger or more mature.

Tips

Spruce are used as specimen trees. The dwarf and slow-growing cultivars can also be used in shrub or mixed borders. These trees look most attractive when allowed to keep their lower branches.

Recommended

Spruce are generally upright, pyramidal trees, but cultivars may be low-growing, wide-spreading or even weeping in habit. *P. abies* (Norway spruce), *P. glauca* (white spruce), *P. omorika* (Serbian spruce), *P. pungens* (Colorado spruce) and their cultivars are popular and commonly available.

Oil-based pesticides such as dormant oil can take the blue out of your blue-needled spruce.

Features: foliage, cones, habit **Habit:** conical or columnar, evergreen tree or shrub **Height:** 60 cm–20 m (24"–65') **Spread:** 60 cm–9 m (24"–30') **Hardiness:** zones 2–8

Sumac

Rhus

Sumacs are unique foliar specimens, ideally suited to contemporary designs where they can exhibit their colourful attributes and architectural form.

Growing

Sumacs develop the best fall colour in **full sun,** but they tolerate partial shade. They prefer soil that is of **average fertility, moist** and **well drained.** Once established, sumacs tolerate drought very well.

Tips

Sumacs can be used to form a specimen group in a shrub or mixed border, on a sloping bank or in a woodland garden. Both male and female plants are needed for fruit to form.

Recommended

R. aromatica (fragrant sumac) forms a low mound of suckering stems and clusters of small yellow flowers in spring. Fuzzy fruit that turns red as it ripens follows the flowers in late spring. The aromatic foliage turns red or purple in fall. Many cultivars are available. (Zones 3–8)

R. glabra (smooth sumac) is an upright, spreading shrub that grows in colonies as it suckers. The green foliage turns orange, red and purple in the fall. Scarlet fruit follows the flowers. A variety of cultivars are available. (Zones 2–8)

R. typhina (*R. hirta,* staghorn sumac) is a suckering, colony-forming shrub with branches covered with velvety fuzz. Fuzzy, yellow, early-summer flowers are followed by hairy, red fruit. The leaves turn stunning shades of yellow, orange and red in fall. (Zones 3–8)

Features: summer and fall foliage, fall fruit **Flower colour:** greenish yellow **Habit:** deciduous low-growing or upright shrub **Height:** 80 cm–3 m (30"–10') **Spread:** 2–4 m (7–13') **Hardiness:** zones 3–8

Viburnum
Viburnum

These plants will look neatest if dead-headed, but this practice will of course prevent fruits from forming. The best fruiting occurs when more than one plant of a species is grown.

Tips

Viburnums can be used in borders and woodland gardens. They are a good choice for planting near decks and patios.

Recommended

Many viburnum species, hybrids and cultivars are available. *V. lantana* (wayfaring tree) is a stout, globe-shaped shrub with leathery, grey-green foliage that turns purplish red in fall. Clusters of creamy white flowers emerge in spring followed by reddish black berries. *V. lentago* (nannyberry) is a large, upright shrub with shiny, green foliage that turns a deep purple-red in the fall. Flat-topped clusters of creamy white flowers emerge in spring, followed by bluish black berries. *V. opulus* (European cranberrybush, Guelder-rose) is a rounded, spreading, deciduous shrub with lacy flower clusters. *V. sargentii* (sargent viburnum) is an upright, globe-shaped shrub that produces ornate foliage and flat-topped clusters of flowers followed by attractive red berries. *V. trilobum* (highbush cranberry) is a dense, rounded shrub with clusters of white flowers followed by edible, red fruit.

Good fall colour, attractive form, shade tolerance, scented flowers and attractive fruit put viburnums in a class by themselves.

Growing

Viburnums grow well in **full sun, partial shade** or **light shade**. The soil should be of **average fertility, moist** and **well drained**. Viburnums tolerate both alkaline and acidic soils.

Only a few species produce edible berries. Most are inedible or eaten only by birds as winter forage.

Features: flowers (some fragrant), summer and fall foliage, fruit **Habit:** bushy or spreading, evergreen, semi-evergreen or deciduous shrub **Height:** 60 cm–6 m (24"–20') **Spread:** 60 cm–3 m (24"–10') **Hardiness:** zones 2–8

Weigela

Weigela

Weigela WINE AND ROSES nestled among lush greenery that complements its purple foliage

Weigelas have been improved through breeding, and specimens with more compact forms, longer flowering periods and greater cold tolerance are now available.

Growing

Weigelas prefer **full sun** but tolerate partial shade. The soil should be **fertile** and **well drained**. These plants will adapt to most well-drained soil conditions.

Tips

Weigelas can be used in shrub or mixed borders, in open woodland gardens and as informal barrier plantings.

Recommended

W. florida is a spreading shrub with arching branches that bears clusters of dark pink flowers. Many hybrids and cultivars are available, including dwarf varieties, red-, pink- or white-flowered varieties and varieties with purple, bronze or yellow foliage.

The trumpet-shaped flowers are attractive to hummingbirds.

Features: late-spring to early-summer flowers, foliage, habit **Habit:** upright or low, spreading, deciduous shrub **Height:** 50 cm–1.5 m (18"–5')
Spread: 50 cm–1.5 m (18"–5')
Hardiness: zones 3–8

Willow

Salix

These fast-growing deciduous shrubs or trees can have colourful or twisted stems and foliage, and they come in a range of growth habits and sizes.

Growing
Willows grow best in **full sun**. Soil should be of **average fertility, moist** and **well drained**, though some of the shrubby species are drought resistant.

Tips
Large tree willows should be reserved for large spaces and look particularly attractive near water features. Smaller willows can be used as small specimen trees or in shrub and mixed borders. Plant small and trailing forms in rock gardens and along retaining walls.

Recommended
There is an endless array of willow tree and shrub species and cultivars to choose from. They can range from creeping, groundcover shrubs with colourful foliage to large shrubs with dense habits and graceful forms. The trees are often quite large and require a grand space to show off their attributes. Check your local garden centre to discover all of the willow possibilities.

Features: summer and fall foliage, stems, habit **Habit:** bushy or arching shrub or spreading or weeping tree **Height:** 30 cm–16 m (12"–55') **Spread:** 1–16 m (3–55') **Hardiness:** zones 2–8

Alexander Mackenzie

Shrub, Explorer Rose

Alexander Mackenzie is known not only for its beauty and scent but also for its outstanding disease resistance. It bears clusters of fragrant, brightly coloured flowers throughout the summer months and well into fall.

Growing
Alexander Mackenzie prefers **full sun**. The soil should be **fertile, rich with organic matter, moist** and **well drained**.

Tips
This rose is extremely hardy, vigorous and highly resistant to powdery mildew and blackspot. It requires very little maintenance. Alexander Mackenzie is suitable as a specimen in a fully exposed location or mixed in with other roses and perennials in a mixed border.

Regular deadheading encourages a longer, more prolific bloom cycle.

Recommended
Rosa 'Alexander Mackenzie' is a tall, upright shrub bearing clusters of fragrant, double flowers. The thorny stems are tinged with hints of reddish purple and carry light green, serrated foliage.

Sir Alexander Mackenzie was a noted explorer and fur trader. In 1793 he became the first European to cross the North American continent and reach the Pacific Ocean.

Features: hardy shrub, mild raspberry-scented flowers bloom in spring and repeat in fall **Flower colour:** deep red with hot pink **Height:** 1.5–2.1 m (5–7') **Spread:** 1.5–2.1 m (5–7') **Hardiness:** zones 3–8

Blanc Double de Coubert

Shrub, Rugosa Rose

Every rose garden should include one of these magnificent rugosa roses. This beautiful rose, over a century old, has a fascinating history and an outstanding reputation.

Growing

This hardy rugosa tolerates light shade but prefers **full sun**. Most soils are adequate but **organically rich, moist, well-drained** soils are best.

Tips

Blanc Double de Coubert is excellent for hedging and borders, and also works well as a specimen. The blossoms are ideal for cutting as well, but cut the stems when they are still partially closed to extend the flowers' vase life.

Recommended

Rosa 'Blanc Double de Coubert' is a moderately vigorous, dense shrub with arching branches. It bears loosely petalled, semi-double, fragrant, white blossoms followed by hips that transform into reddish orange spheres and stand out among the stunning fall foliage.

Blanc Double de Coubert is highly resistant to disease.

The soft petals are easily marked by rain, which may cause the flowers to appear spent not long after they open.

Features: hardiness; strongly scented, early-summer flowers that repeat in fall
Flower colour: white **Height:** 1.2–2.1 m (4–7') **Spread:** 1.2–2.1 m (4–7')
Hardiness: zones 3–8

Hansa

Shrub, Rugosa Rose

Hansa, first introduced in 1905, is one of the most durable, long-lived and versatile roses.

Growing

Hansa grows best in **full sun**. Soil should preferably be **average to fertile, humus rich, slightly acidic, moist** and **well drained,** but this durable rose adapts to most soils, from sandy to silty clay. Remove a few of the oldest canes every few years to keep plants blooming vigorously.

Tips

Rugosa roses like Hansa make good additions to mixed borders and beds, and can also be used as hedges or as specimens.

They are often used on steep banks to prevent soil erosion. Their prickly branches deter people from walking across flower beds and compacting the soil.

Recommended

Rosa 'Hansa' is a bushy shrub with arching canes and leathery, deeply veined, bright green leaves. The double flowers are produced all summer, and the bright orange hips persist into winter. Other rugosa roses include '**Blanc Double de Coubert**,' which produces white, double flowers all summer.

Features: dense, arching habit; clove-scented, early-summer to fall flowers; orange-red hips
Flower colour: mauve purple or mauve red
Height: 1.2–1.5 m (4–5') **Spread:** 1.5–1.8 m (5–6') **Hardiness:** zones 2–8

Henry Hudson

Shrub, Explorer Rose

The explorer roses were developed by Agriculture Canada to be cold hardy and disease resistant, making them ideal for Canadian gardens. All the roses in this series have been named after explorers.

Henry Hudson was introduced in 1976 and has proven to be easy to maintain, hardy and resistant to mildew and blackspot.

Growing

Henry Hudson grows best in **full sun,** but tolerates some afternoon shade. Soil should be **average to fertile, humus rich, slightly acidic, moist** and **well drained**. Deadhead to keep plants tidy.

Tips

With its thorny, impenetrable growth, Henry Hudson makes an attractive barrier plant, hedge or groundcover. It spreads by suckers and can be used on banks to prevent soil erosion. It also looks attractive in mixed beds or borders.

Recommended

Rosa 'Henry Hudson' is a spreading, rounded shrub with bright green foliage and semi-double flowers that bloom profusely all summer. Roses in the explorer series come in a variety of flower colours and sizes, including climbers.

Features: rounded habit; clove-scented, early-summer to fall flowers
Flower colour: white **Height:** 60–90 cm (24–36") **Spread:** 60 cm–1.2 m (24"–5') **Hardiness:** zones 2–8

Hope For Humanity

Shrub, Parkland Rose

Introduced in 1995, Hope for Humanity was named in honour of the 100th anniversary of the Canadian Red Cross Society.

Growing

Hope for Humanity grows best in **full sun**. Soil should be **fertile, humus rich, slightly acidic, moist** and **well drained**. Its foliage is resistant to mildew and rust, but somewhat susceptible to blackspot.

Tips

This small, attractive plant makes a good addition to a mixed bed or border, and it is attractive when planted in groups of three or more. Its small stature also makes it a popular choice for containers and large planters, though some winter protection may be needed for plants not grown directly in the ground.

Recommended

Rosa 'Hope for Humanity' is a compact, low-growing shrub with glossy, dark green foliage and double flowers produced over a long period in summer. The Parkland rose series boasts a wide range of flower colours, some of which are uncommon in hardy shrub roses.

The hardy Parkland roses were developed in Morden, Manitoba for use in prairie gardens.

Features: compact habit; lightly scented, mid-summer to fall flowers **Flower colour:** blood red with a small white spot at petal base and a white or yellow spot on the outer margin of each petal **Height:** 60 cm (24") **Spread:** 60 cm (24") **Hardiness:** zones 3–8

Jens Munk

Shrub, Explorer Rose

This rose is extremely tough, highly disease resistant and drought tolerant. It requires very little to no maintenance.

The American Rose Society doesn't bestow the 'highly recommended' classification on just any rose. This tough and dependable explorer rose is favoured by both ARS rose enthusiasts and northern gardeners.

Growing

Jens Munk grows best in **full to partial sun**. It prefers a **fertile, moist but well-drained**, **slightly acidic** soil.

Tips

With its vast number of prickles, Jens Munk makes an impenetrable, medium-sized hedge. It blends beautifully into mixed beds and borders or works well as a specimen.

Recommended

Rosa 'Jens Munk' grows vigorously into a rounded, dense shrub. It has a sprawling and unshapely form when young but evens out with maturity. Bright red hips follow the semi-double flowers. The wrinkly, shiny foliage turns a beautiful yellow-orange hue in the fall.

Features: upright habit; spicy-scented, summer blossoms that repeat in fall
Flower colour: medium pink, purple
Height: 1.5–2.1 m (5–7')
Spread: 1.2–1.5 m (4–5')
Hardiness: zones 3–8

John Cabot

Shrub, Explorer Rose

This rose was named after the first European since the Vikings to explore the North American mainland and search for the Northwest Passage. It is considered one of the best explorer roses, exhibiting semi-double clusters of blooms that fade to pale pink over time.

Growing

John Cabot requires **partial to full sun**. The soil should be **average to fertile, slightly acidic, humus rich, moist** and **well drained**.

Tips

This variety works best trained as a climber but it can be pruned into a smaller specimen once it has finished flowering. Train the branches to climb on a decorative support such as a pergola, archway, trellis or obelisk.

Recommended

Rosa 'John Cabot' is a vigorous and tough rose that requires little maintenance and has good resistance to blackspot and powdery mildew. The prominent yellow stamens stand out among the cupped petals and light green foliage. The flower colour can range from deep pink to reddish purple.

Features: sweetly scented, mid-summer blossoms that repeat in fall
Flower colour: deep, vivid magenta pink
Height: 2.4–3 m (8–10') **Spread:** 1.5–1.8 m (5–6') **Hardiness:** zones 3–8

John Franklin

Shrub, Explorer Rose

This rose was named after a well-known British naval officer and northern explorer. Franklin is remembered for his expeditions and for the highly publicized 12-year search for him and his lost ships in the mid-1800s.

John Franklin has a slightly different flowering habit than other explorer roses. It is an everblooming rose, meaning that rather than repeat blooming, it blooms continuously from summer to fall. The bright red flowers keep coming, rain or shine, until cool fall days finally slow them down.

Growing

John Franklin tolerates shade but prefers **partial to full sun**. The soil should be a **fertile, well-drained, moisture-holding loam** with at least five percent organic matter.

Tips

Its compact, bushy form makes this rose useful for hedging, borders and smaller gardens. John Franklin is ideal for those tight spaces that need a punch of colour.

Recommended

Rosa '**John Franklin**' bears tight buds that open to semi-double flowers. The small, fringed flowers are borne in abundant, large clusters of 30 or more. The leaves are serrated and dark green with touches of burgundy around the edges.

Features: compact, bushy form; lightly scented blossoms that bloom from spring to fall **Flower colour:** medium red **Height:** 1.2–1.5 m (4–5') **Spread:** 1.2 m (4') **Hardiness:** zones 3–8

Martin Frobisher

Shrub, Explorer Rose

In 1968, Martin Frobisher became the first rose to be introduced in the Canadian explorer series. It has the appearance of an old rose but has a few unique physical features—the older growth is covered in reddish brown bark, the upper portions of the branches are spineless and it does not form hips.

Growing

Martin Frobisher prefers at least five or six hours of **full sun** daily. The soil should be **well drained**, **slightly acidic**, **humus rich** and **moist**.

Unlike most explorer roses, hips do not form on this rose once the flowers are finished.

Features: tall, upright form; intensely scented, early-summer blossoms that repeat in fall
Flower colour: pale pink **Height:** 1.5–1.8 m (5–6') **Spread:** 1.2–1.5 m (4–5')
Hardiness: zones 2–8

Tips

This upright shrub rose works well in mixed borders but also makes an effective specimen.

Recommended

Rosa 'Martin Frobisher' bears intensely fragrant, double flowers that open from well-shaped buds. It is a vigorous, dense, compact, well-proportioned, pillar-shaped shrub. Dark red, smooth stems display wrinkly, greyish green leaves.

Morden Blush

Shrub, Parkland Rose

Its pale pink, delicate blooms may lead you to believe that this rose is tender, but Morden Blush tolerates drought and extreme temperatures. It is heat and cold hardy, disease resistant and vigorous.

Growing

Morden Blush grows best in **full to partial sun.** It prefers a deep, **well-drained loam** that is **rich in organic matter** and **slightly acidic.**

Tips

The blooms are frequently used for corsages and bouquets; landscape uses include mass plantings, borders and mixed beds. Place it in a well-ventilated area and water at the base of the plant in the morning to prevent the onset of disease.

Recommended

Rosa 'Morden Blush' is a small shrub with attractive buds that open flat into fully double sprays of rosette-shaped clusters. Each petal is in-folded, forming into a muddled, button-shaped centre.

Features: small, compact size; tea-scented, late-spring blossoms that continue throughout fall **Flower colour:** pale pink **Height:** 60–90 cm (24–36") **Spread:** 60–90 cm (24–36") **Hardiness:** zones 2b–8

Morden Fireglow

Shrub, Parkland Rose

This rose is truly one of my favourites. One of the Parkland series, this hardy specimen bears flowers that are neither red nor orange—a colour unlike that of any other hardy shrub rose.

Growing

Morden Fireglow prefers at least five to six hours of **full sun** per day. The soil should be **moist, well drained, slightly acidic** and **organically rich.**

Tips

Morden Fireglow will stand out among a variety of sun-loving plants, making it ideal for mixed beds and borders. Cut the stems while the flowers are still buds to extend the longevity of the cut flowers in bouquets.

Recommended

Rosa 'Morden Fireglow' is an upright shrub that bears double blossoms formed in loosely cupped sprays. The large, globular hips that form in fall remain on the plant well into the following spring.

This plant is considered self-cleaning because the petals fall cleanly from the plant once they've finished blooming.

Features: unique flower colour, upright form, early-summer flowers that repeat in fall
Flower colour: deep scarlet red with orange
Height: 60 cm–1.2 m (24"–4') **Spread:** 60–90 cm (24–36") **Hardiness:** zones 2b–8

Morden Ruby

Shrub, Parkland Rose

Morden Ruby blooms are a unique blend of dark and light flecks and pink tones. Some of the flowers change to solid colours or fade with age, but overall Morden Ruby flowers are notably different from other Parkland series rose blooms.

Growing

Morden Ruby grows best in **full sun**. The soil should be **slightly acidic, moist** but **well drained** and **humus rich**.

The very long-lasting flowers are suitable for cutting and arrangements.

Tips

Morden Ruby is suitable for just about any garden setting including cottage gardens. It can be left as a beautiful specimen or mixed with a variety of blooming shrubs and perennials. Plant in large groups for a strong visual impact.

Morden Ruby is naturally vigorous and somewhat lanky. If you want a bushier plant, prune hard in early spring, before the plant fully leafs out, and cut the longest rangy canes to the ground.

Recommended

Rosa '**Morden Ruby**' bears strong stems that support shiny, dark green leaves. Double clusters of lightly scented flowers open from oval, reddish buds in late spring.

Features: compact, upright form; blossoms are borne in spring and again in fall **Flower colour:** mottled, light and dark pink blend **Height:** 90 cm–1.2 m (3–4') **Spread:** 1.2 m (4') **Hardiness:** zones 2–8

Morden Snowbeauty

Shrub, Parkland Rose

Morden Snowbeauty is the only white bloomer of the Parkland series. It is also one of the most recent series introductions, released in 1998. This extremely hardy specimen bears a large quantity of blooms in early summer, with intermittent flowers thereafter.

Growing

Morden Snowbeauty is tolerant of **partial shade** but prefers **full sun. Well-drained** but **moist, slightly acidic, humus-rich** soil is best.

Tips

Planted en masse, these white roses look strikingly beautiful. Morden Snowbeauty is also ideal for borders or left as a prolific specimen. Its foliage is healthy, highly resistant to disease and requires very little care or maintenance.

Recommended

Rosa 'Morden Snowbeauty' bears rather large, semi-double clusters of flowers exposing bright yellow stamens. This low-spreading shrub is covered in shiny, dark green, healthy foliage.

A heavy, second flush of blooms can be encouraged with a little deadheading and regular fertilizing.

Features: small stature; white blossoms emerge in early summer and again in fall **Flower colour:** white **Height:** 30 cm–1 m (12"–3') **Spread:** 40 cm–1.2 m (18"–4') **Hardiness:** zones 2b–8

Morden Sunrise

Shrub, Parkland Rose

Morden Sunrise is the most adorable semi-double rose I've seen in recent years. Its 1999 introduction was highly anticipated, and the public received it very well. It remains as popular today as it was in the year of its introduction.

Growing

Morden Sunrise prefers **full sun**. The soil should be **well drained** but **moist, slightly acidic** and **rich with organic matter**.

Tips

This rose is ideal for borders and mixed beds, or it can be grown as a specimen. Morden Sunrise is a colourful addition to just about any garden setting.

Recommended

Rosa 'Morden Sunrise' is a compact shrub formed by erect stems, dense foliage and semi-double flowers. The first yellow variety in the Parkland series, it has a clean and fresh look, with blooms in tones of apricot and yellow along with attractive, shiny, dark green leaves.

Cooler temperatures cause the flower colour to intensify, while hotter weather results in paler, softer tones.

This rose, bred for harsh winters, also performs beautifully in areas with mild winters.

Features: compact size; lightly scented, apricot flowers that emerge in early summer and again in fall **Flower colour:** apricot yellow **Height:** 60–75 cm (24–30") **Spread:** 60–75 cm (24–30") **Hardiness:** zones 3–8

Red-Leafed Rose

Species Rose

This rose thrives where most plants could not survive. The starry, pink blossoms make a striking contrast with the violet-tinted foliage. The foliage sometimes appears to change colour depending on the degree of sun exposure.

Growing

Red-leafed rose tolerates shade but prefers **full sun**. Most soils are fine but **well drained**, **moist**, **slightly acidic** soil is best. Keep this species under control with regular pruning, which will encourage new and colourful shoots.

Tips

Red-leafed rose makes an ideal hedge because of its vigorous nature and arching, thorny, purple stems. Its burgundy hips and maroon stems lend colour to a stark winter landscape. It also makes a splendid specimen.

Recommended

Rosa glauca is extremely popular among rosarians and novice gardeners alike because it is so hardy and disease resistant. Its flowers are followed by clusters of small, rounded, dark red hips that remain on the shrub well into the following spring.

Also called: Rosa glauca **Features:** tall, upright form; single flowers emerge in late spring and continue to bloom until summer **Flower colour:** mauve pink, white centres **Height:** 1.8–3 m (6–10') **Spread:** 1.5–1.8 m (5–6') **Hardiness:** zones 2–8

William Baffin

Shrub, Explorer Rose

Tough and versatile, hardy and vigorous, this rose meets all expectations. William Baffin is highly disease resistant and requires very little to no maintenance. It is thought to be the best shrub or climbing rose for colder regions.

Growing

William Baffin prefers **full sun** but tolerates afternoon shade. **Average to fertile, slightly acidic** soil that's **rich with organic matter** works best. The soil should also be **moist** and **well drained**.

Tips

William Baffin is tall enough to be trained as a climber or pillar rose. It is hardy enough to remain on a trellis, arbour or pergola in the coldest of winters, and does not need pruning or any special winter protection.

Recommended

Rosa 'William Baffin' bears semi-double flowers borne in clusters of 30 or more. Glossy, medium-green foliage is vigorously produced in dense mounds on wiry, stiff stems.

This rose was named after the famous explorer who discovered Lancaster Sound in northern Canada while he searched for the Northwest Passage in 1616.

Features: vigorous, hardy climber with lightly scented, summer flowers that repeat in fall **Flower colour:** deep pink **Height:** 2.4–3 m (8–10') **Spread:** 1.5–1.8 m (5–6') **Hardiness:** zones 2–8

Bittersweet

Celastrus

Bittersweet is a rough-and-tumble, low-maintenance, woody climber that will lend a wild look to your garden. Highly decorative clusters of fruit burst forth in the fall.

Growing

Bittersweet grows well in **full sun** and tolerates partial shade. It prefers **poor soil** but adapts to almost any **well-drained** soil.

Male and female flowers usually bloom on separate plants. Both sexes, planted in close proximity, are needed for fruit production. Bittersweet is often sold with a male and a female plant in one pot. Water them well.

Tips

Bittersweet belongs at the edge of a woodland garden and in a naturalized area. It quickly covers fences, arbours, trellises, posts and walls. As a groundcover it can mask rubble and tree stumps, and it effectively controls erosion on hard-to-maintain slopes. All parts of bittersweet are said to be poisonous.

This vine can damage or kill young trees or shrubs if it's allowed to twine around their stems.

Recommended

C. scandens (American bittersweet, staff vine) is a vigorous, twining vine with dark green, glossy foliage that turns bright yellow in fall. Small, yellow-green to whitish flowers bloom in late spring followed by showy fruit. '**Indian Brave**' and '**Indian Maid**,' the male and female cultivar pair, are hardier than the species.

Generally, one male plant will pollinate six to nine female plants. The subsequent berry production is very attractive to birds.

Also called: American bittersweet **Features:** fast growth, twining stems, fruit, fall colour **Height:** 2–3 m (6^1/$_2$–10') **Spread:** 90 cm–1.8 m (3–6') **Hardiness:** zones 3–8

Black-Eyed Susan Vine

Thunbergia

The blooms are actually trumpet shaped, with the dark centres forming a tube.

Black-eyed Susan vine is a useful flowering vine whose simple flowers dot the plant, giving it a cheerful, welcoming appearance.

Growing

Black-eyed Susan vines do well in **full sun, partial shade** or **light shade**. Grow in **fertile, moist, well-drained** soil that is high in **organic matter**.

Tips

Black-eyed Susan vines can be trained to twine up and around fences, walls, trees and shrubs. They are also attractive trailing down from the top of a rock garden or rock wall or growing in mixed containers and hanging baskets.

Recommended

T. alata is a vigorous, twining climber. It bears yellow flowers, often with dark centres, in summer and fall. Cultivars with large flowers in yellow, orange or white are available.

T. grandiflora (skyflower vine, blue trumpet vine) is less commonly available than *T. alata*. It tends to bloom late, in early to mid-fall. This twining climber bears stunning, pale violet blue flowers. '**Alba**' has white flowers.

Features: twining habit; yellow, orange, violet blue or creamy white, dark-centred flowers
Height: 1.5 m (5') or more **Spread:** 1.5 m (5') or more **Hardiness:** tender perennial treated as an annual

Clematis
Clematis

There are so many species, hybrids and cultivars of clematis that it is possible to have one in bloom all season.

Growing
Clematis plants prefer **full sun** but tolerate partial shade. The soil should be **fertile, humus rich, moist** and **well drained**. These vines enjoy warm, sunny weather, but the roots prefer to be cool. A thick layer of mulch or a planting of low, shade-providing perennials will protect the tender roots. Clematis are quite cold hardy but will fare best when protected from winter wind. The rootball of vining clematis should be planted about 5 cm (2") beneath the surface of the soil.

Tips
Clematis vines can climb up structures such as trellises, railings, fences and arbours. They can also grow over shrubs and up trees and can be used as groundcover.

Recommended
There are many species, hybrids and cultivars of clematis. The flower forms, blooming times and sizes of the plants can vary. Check with your local garden centre to see what is available.

Features: twining habit; blue, purple, pink, yellow, red or white, early- to late-summer flowers; decorative seedheads **Height:** 3–5 m (10–17') or more **Spread:** 1.5 m (5') or more **Hardiness:** zones 3–8

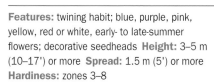

Cup-and-Saucer Vine
Cobaea

Cup-and-saucer vine is a vigorous climber native to Mexico that produces frilly, purple flowers from spring until frost.

Growing
Cup-and-saucer vine prefers **full sun**. The soil should be **well drained** and of **average fertility**. This plant is fond of hot weather and will do best if planted in a sheltered site with southern exposure. Set the seeds on edge when planting them, and barely cover them with soil.

Tips
Grow this vine up a trellis, over an arbour or along a chain-link fence. Cup-and-saucer vine requires a sturdy support in order to climb. It uses grabbing hooks to climb so won't be able to grow up a wall without something to grab. It can be trained to fill almost any space. In a hanging basket the vine will climb the hanger and spill over the edges.

Recommended
C. scandens is a vigorous climbing vine with flowers that are creamy green when they open and mature to deep purple. **Var. *alba*** has white flowers.

Also called: cathedral bells **Features:** purple or white flowers, clinging habit, long blooming period **Height:** 3–6 m (10–20') **Spread:** 3–6 m (10–20') **Hardiness:** tender perennial treated as an annual

Hardy Kiwi
Actinidia

Hardy kiwi is handsome in its simplicity. Its lush green leaves, vigour and adaptability make it very useful, especially in difficult sites.

Growing
Hardy kiwi vines grow best in **full sun**. The soil should be **fertile** and **well drained**. These plants require shelter from strong winds.

Tips
These vines need a sturdy structure to twine around. Pergolas, arbours and sufficiently large and sturdy fences provide good support. Given a trellis against a wall, a tree or some other upright structure, hardy kiwis will twine upward all summer. They can also be grown in containers.

Hardy kiwi vines can grow uncontrollably. Don't be afraid to prune them back if they get out of hand.

Recommended
There are two hardy kiwi vines commonly grown in Canadian gardens. *A. arguta* (hardy kiwi, bower actinidia) has dark green, heart-shaped leaves, white flowers and smooth-skinned, greenish yellow, edible fruit. *A. kolomikta* (variegated kiwi vine, kolomikta actinidia) has green leaves strongly variegated with pink and white, smooth-skinned, greenish yellow, edible fruit and white flowers.

Both a male and a female vine must be present for fruit to be produced. The plants are often sold in pairs.

Features: early-summer flowers, edible fruit, twining habit **Height:** 4.5–9 m (15–30') to indefinite **Spread:** 4.5–9 m (15–30') to indefinite **Hardiness:** zones 3–8

Honeysuckle

Lonicera

Honeysuckles can be rampant twining vines, but with careful consideration and placement they won't overrun your garden. The fragrance of the flowers makes any effort worthwhile.

Growing

Honeysuckles grow well in **full sun** or **partial shade.** The soil should be **average to fertile, humus rich, moist** and **well drained.**

Tips

Honeysuckle can be trained to grow up a trellis, fence, arbour or other structure. In a large container near a porch it will ramble over the edges of the pot and up the railings with reckless abandon.

Recommended

There are dozens of honeysuckle species, hybrids and cultivars. Check with your local garden centre to see what is available. The following are two popular species.

L. x *brownii* (scarlet trumpet honeysuckle) produces blue-green, rounded leaves and clusters of fiery, tubular flowers on the tips of twining stems. Many cultivars are available. (Zones 3–8)

L. sempervirens (trumpet honeysuckle, coral honeysuckle) bears orange or red flowers in late spring and early summer. Many cultivars and hybrids are available. (Zones 4–8)

Honeysuckle flowers are often scented and attract hummingbirds as well as bees and other pollinating insects.

Lonicera comes in both the hardy vine and shrub form. See page 88 for the honeysuckle shrub.

Features: late-spring and early-summer flowers; twining habit; fruit **Height:** 1.8–4.5 m (6–15')
Spread: 1.8–4.5 m (6–15')
Hardiness: zones 3–8

Hops

Humulus

*I*f you sit nearby for an afternoon, you might actually see your hops vine grow.

Growing

Hops grow best in **full sun**. The soil should be **average to fertile, humus rich, moist** and **well drained**, though established plants will adapt to most conditions as long as they are well watered for the first few years.

Tips

Hops will quickly twine around any sturdy support to create a screen or shade a patio or deck. Provide a pergola, arbour, porch rail or even a telephone pole for hops to grow up. Most trellises are too delicate for this vigorous grower.

Recommended

H. lupulus is a fast-growing, twining vine with rough-textured, bright green leaves and stems. The fragrant, cone-like flowers—used to flavour beer—are produced only on the female plants. A cultivar with golden yellow foliage is available.

Hops are true perennials; each year the plant sends up shoots from ground level. The previous year's growth will need to be cleared away.

Features: twining habit; dense growth; cone-like, late-summer flowers **Height:** 3–6 m (10–20') **Spread:** 3–6 m (10–20') **Hardiness:** zones 3–8

Morning Glory

Ipomoea

Morning glory will embellish a chain-link fence, a wire topiary structure or any object thin enough to twine its tendrils around. Once established, stand back—this vine grows fast.

Growing

Grow morning glory in **full sun** in **light, well-drained** soil of **poor fertility**. It will tolerate any type of soil. Soak seeds for 24 hours before sowing. Start seeds in individual peat pots if sowing indoors. Plant in late spring.

Tips

Morning glory can be grown anywhere: on fences, walls, trees, trellises and arbours. As a groundcover, it will cover any obstacles it encounters.

Morning glory needs objects such as wire or twine in order to climb. Wide fence posts, walls or other broad objects are too large.

Recommended

I. alba (moonflower) has sweet-scented, white flowers that open at night.

I. purpurea (common morning glory) bears trumpet-shaped flowers in purple, blue, pink or white.

I. tricolor (morning glory) produces purple or blue flowers with white centres. Many cultivars are available.

Features: fast growth **Habit:** herbaceous, twining vine or groundcover **Flower colour:** white, blue, pink or purple and variegated **Height:** 3–3.5 m (10–12') **Spread:** 30–60 cm (12–24") **Hardiness:** treat as an annual

Passion Flower

Passiflora

Passion flowers are exotic and mesmerizing. They grow and bloom prolifically outdoors in the summer and, moved indoors, may even sport a flower or two during the winter.

Growing

Grow passion flower in **full sun** or **partial shade**. This plant prefers **well-drained**, **moist** soil of **average fertility**. Keep it sheltered from wind and cold.

Tips

Passion flower is a popular addition to mixed containers, and it makes an unusual focal point near a door. This plant is actually a fast-growing, woody climber that is grown as an annual.

Recommended

P. caerulea bears unusual purple-banded, purple-white flowers all summer.

Small, round fruits follow after the exotic flowers. The fruits are edible but not very tasty.

Passion flower can be composted at the end of summer or cut back and brought inside to live in a bright room over winter.

Features: exotic, colourful flowers; twining habit; ornate foliage **Flower colour:** white or pale pink petals with blue or purple bands **Height:** up to 9 m (30') **Spread:** variable **Hardiness:** treat as an annual

Scarlet Runner Bean

Phaseolus

Scarlet runner beans are both functional and beautiful. They'll scramble up a support in no time at all, blooming throughout the summer months and producing buckets of beans good enough to eat.

Growing

Scarlet runner bean prefers to grow in **full sun** in **well-drained, fertile, moist** soil. Provide adequate water.

Tips

Scarlet runner bean is a twining climber and will need something to climb, such as a trellis, arbour or post. Attach some form of lattice or netting if you want scarlet runner bean to grow up a fence or building.

Recommended

P. coccineus is a fast-growing, twining vine that grows to a height of 2–2.7 m (6 ½–9'). It bears clusters of scarlet red flowers in summer. Dark green, edible pods follow flowering. Cultivars are available with red and white bicoloured and solid white flowers.

These plants are at home in the flower garden as well as the vegetable garden. The dark green pods are edible; they are tender when young but tougher with age. Pick the pods just after the flowers fade for best taste in a stir-fry.

Features: scarlet flowers, twining habit, fruit
Flower colour: red **Height:** 1.8–2.4 m (6–8')
Spread: 2.4–3 m (8–10') **Hardiness:** treat as an annual

Sweet Pea

Lathyrus

Sweet peas are among the most enchanting annuals. Their fragrance is intoxicating and the flowers in double tones and shimmering shades look like no other annual in the garden.

Growing

Sweet peas prefer **full sun** but tolerate light shade. The soil should be **fertile,** high in **organic matter, moist** and **well drained.** The plants tolerate light frost.

Soak seeds in water for 24 hours or nick them with a nail file before planting them. Planting a second crop of sweet peas about a month after the first one will ensure a longer blooming period. Deadhead all spent blooms.

Tips

Sweet peas will grow up poles, trellises and fences or over rocks. They cling by wrapping tendrils around whatever they are growing up, so they do best when they have a rough surface, chain-link fence, small twigs or a net to cling to.

Recommended

There are many cultivars of **L. odoratus** available, though many are now small and bushy rather than climbing. '**Bouquet**' is a tall, climbing variety with flowers in a wide range of colours.

Newer sweet pea cultivars often have less fragrant flowers than old-fashioned cultivars. Look for heritage varieties to enjoy the most fragrant flowers.

Features: clinging habit; pink, red, purple, lavender, blue, salmon, pale yellow, peach, white or bicoloured summer flowers **Height:** 30 cm–1.8 m (12"–6') **Spread:** 15–30 cm (6–12")
Hardiness: hardy annual

Virginia Creeper
Parthenocissus

Virginia creeper and Boston ivy are handsome vines that establish quickly and provide an air of age and permanence, even on new structures.

Virginia creeper can cover the sides of a building and keep it cool in summer. Cut it back to keep windows and doors accessible.

Growing
These vines grow well in any light, from **full sun to full shade**. The soil should be **fertile** and **well drained**. The plants will adapt to clay or sandy soils.

Tips
Virginia creepers can cover an entire building, given enough time. They do not require support because they have clinging rootlets that adhere to just about any surface, even smooth wood, vinyl or metal. Give the plants lots of space and let them cover a wall, fence or arbour.

Recommended
These two species are very similar, except for the shape of the leaves.

P. quinquefolia (Virginia creeper, woodbine) has dark green foliage. Each leaf, divided into five leaflets, turns flame red in fall. **P. quinquefolia var. engelmannii** (Engelman ivy) is another self-clinging variety but unlike the species, it attaches itself to supports or surfaces with adhesive pads rather than tendrils. It is equally as colourful and vigorous but far more resistant to powdery mildew than the species. This variety should not be grown against wooden structures or surfaces that will require maintenance.

Features: summer and fall foliage, clinging habit **Height:** 9–21 m (30–70') **Spread:** 9–21 m (30–70') **Hardiness:** zones 3–8

Calla Lily

Zantedeschia

This beautiful, exotic-looking plant was only available as a cut flower in the past. The introduction of new cultivars, however, has made it more readily available and worth planting.

Growing

Calla lilies grow best in **full sun**. The soil should be **fertile, humus rich** and **moist**. Callas grown in containers can be brought indoors for winter. Reduce watering in winter; keep the soil just moist.

Tips

Calla lilies are ideal additions to mixed beds and borders, and work well as container specimens.

Rather than moving large, cumbersome plants, it is sometimes easier to remove small divisions in fall and transfer them indoors over winter.

Recommended

Z. aethiopica (white arum lily, white calla) forms a clump of arrow-shaped, glossy green leaves. It bears white flowers from late spring to mid-summer. Several cultivars are available.

Z. elliottiana (yellow calla, golden calla) forms a basal clump of white-spotted, dark green, heart-shaped leaves. It grows 60–90 cm (24–36") tall and spreads 20–30 cm (8–12"). This species bears yellow flowers in summer and is a parent plant of many popular hybrids.

Although they grow quite large, calla lilies can be grown as houseplants all year-round, but they benefit from spending summer outdoors.

Features: flowers, foliage **Height:** 40–90 cm (16–36") **Spread:** 20–60 cm (8–24") **Hardiness:** zone 8; grown as an annual

Daffodil

Narcissus

Many gardeners automatically think of large, yellow, trumpet-shaped flowers when they think of daffodils, but there is a lot of variety in colour, form and size among the daffodils.

Growing

Daffodils grow best in **full sun** or **light, dappled shade**. The soil should be **average to fertile, moist** and **well drained**. Bulbs should be planted in fall, 5–20 cm (2–8") deep, depending on the size of the bulb. The bigger the bulb the deeper it should be planted. A rule of thumb is to measure the bulb from top to bottom and multiply that number by three to know how deep to plant it.

Tips

Daffodils are often planted where they can be left to naturalize, in the light shade beneath a tree or in a woodland garden. In mixed beds and borders, the faded leaves are hidden by other plants' summer foliage.

Recommended

Many species, hybrids and cultivars of daffodils are available. Flowers come in shades of white, yellow, peach, orange and pink, and may be bicoloured. Flowers measure 4–15 cm (1½–6") across, borne solitary or in clusters. There are 12 flower form categories.

The cup in the centre of a daffodil is called the corona, and the group of petals that surrounds the corona is called the perianth.

Features: spring flowers **Height:** 10–60 cm (4–24") **Spread:** 10–30 cm (4–12") **Hardiness:** zones 3–8

Gladiolus

Gladiolus

Perhaps best known as a cut flower, gladiolus adds an air of extravagance to the garden.

Growing

Gladiolus grows best in **full sun** but tolerates partial shade. The soil should be **fertile, humus rich, moist** and **well drained**. Flower spikes may need staking and shelter from the wind to prevent the flower spike from blowing over.

Plant corms in spring, 10–15 cm (4–6") deep, once soil has warmed. Corms can also be started early indoors. Plant a few corms each week for about a month to prolong the blooming period.

Tips

Planted in groups in beds and borders, gladiolus makes a bold statement. Corms can also be pulled up in fall and stored in damp peat moss in a cool, frost-free location for the winter.

Recommended

G. x *hortulanus* is a huge group of hybrids. Gladiolus flowers come in almost every imaginable shade, except blue. Plants are commonly grouped in three classifications: **Grandiflorus** is the best known; each corm produces a single spike of large, often ruffled flowers. **Nanus**, the hardiest group, survives in zone 3 with protection and produces several spikes of up to seven flowers. **Primulinus** produces a single spike of up to 23 flowers that grow more spaced out than those of the grandiflorus.

Over 10,000 cultivars of gladiolus have been developed.

Features: brightly coloured mid- to late-summer flowers **Height:** 45 cm–1.8 m (18"–6') **Spread:** 15–30 cm (6–12") **Hardiness:** zone 8; grown as an annual

Lily
Lilium

Decorative clusters of large, richly coloured blooms grace these tall plants. Flowers are produced at differing times of the season, depending on the hybrid, and it is possible to have lilies blooming all season if a variety of cultivars are chosen.

Growing

Lilies grow best in **full sun**, but like to have their **roots shaded**. The soil should be rich in **organic matter, fertile, moist** and **well drained**.

Tips

Lilies are often grouped in beds and borders and can be naturalized in woodland gardens and near water features. These plants are narrow but tall; group at least three plants together to create some volume.

Recommended

The many species, hybrids and cultivars available are grouped by type. Visit your local garden centre to see what is available. The following are two popular groups of lilies. **Asiatic hybrids** bear clusters of flowers in early summer or mid-summer and are available in a wide range of colours. **Oriental hybrids** bear clusters of large, fragrant flowers in mid- and late summer. Colours are usually white, pink or red.

Lily bulbs should be planted in fall before the first frost, but they can also be planted in spring if bulbs are available.

Also called: Oriental lily, Asiatic lily
Features: early, mid- or late-season flowers in shades of orange, yellow, peach, pink, purple, red, white **Height:** 60 cm–1.5 m (24"–5') **Spread:** 30 cm (12")
Hardiness: zones 2–8

Ornamental Onion

Allium

Ornamental onions, with their striking, ball-like or loose, nodding clusters of flowers, are sure to attract attention in the garden.

Growing

Ornamental onions grow best in **full sun**. The soil should be **average to fertile, moist** and **well drained**. Plant bulbs in fall, 5–10 cm (2–4") deep, depending on size of bulb.

Tips

Ornamental onions are best planted in groups in a bed or border where they can be left to naturalize. Most will self-seed when left to their own devices. The foliage, which tends to fade just as the plants come into flower, can be hidden with groundcover or a low, bushy companion plant.

Recommended

Several ornamental onion species, hybrids and cultivars have gained popularity for their decorative pink, purple, white, yellow, blue or maroon flowers. These include *A. aflatunense,* with dense, globe-like clusters of lavender flowers; *A. caeruleum* (blue globe onion), with globe-like clusters of blue flowers; *A. cernuum* (nodding or wild onion), with loose, drooping clusters of pink flowers; and *A. giganteum* (giant onion), a big plant up to 2 m (6') tall, with large, globe-shaped clusters of pinky purple flowers.

Though the leaves have an onion scent when bruised, the flowers are often sweetly fragrant.

Features: summer flowers, cylindrical or strap-shaped leaves **Height:** 30 cm–2 m (12"–7') **Spread:** 5–30 cm (2–12") **Hardiness:** zones 3–8

Tulip
Tulipa

Tulips, with their beautiful and often garishly coloured flowers, are a welcome sight in the warm days of spring.

Growing

Tulips grow best in **full sun**. The flowers tend to bend toward the light in partial or light shade. The soil should be **fertile** and **well drained**. Plant bulbs in fall, 10–15 cm (4–6") deep, depending on the size of bulb. Bulbs that have been cold treated can be planted in spring. Though tulips can repeat bloom, many hybrids perform best if planted new each year. Species and older cultivars naturalize well.

Tips

Tulips provide the best display when mass planted or planted in groups in flowerbeds and borders. They can also be grown in containers and forced to bloom early in pots indoors. Some of the species and older cultivars can be naturalized in meadow and wildflower gardens.

Recommended

There are about 100 species of tulips and thousands of hybrids and cultivars. They are generally divided into 15 groups based on bloom time and flower appearance. They come in dozens of shades, with many bicoloured or multi-coloured varieties. Blue is the only shade not available. Check with your local garden centre in early fall for the best selection.

Features: spring flowers **Height:** 15–75 cm (6–30") **Spread:** 5–20 cm (2–8") **Hardiness:** zones 3–8

Basil

Ocimum

The sweet, fragrant leaves of fresh basil add a delicious licorice-like flavour to salads and tomato-based dishes.

Growing

Basil grows best in a **warm, sheltered** location in **full sun**. The soil should be **fertile, moist** and **well drained**. Pinch tips regularly to encourage bushy growth. Plant out or direct sow seed after frost danger has passed in spring.

Tips

Though basil grows best in a warm spot outdoors, it can be grown successfully in a pot by a bright window indoors to provide you with fresh leaves all year.

Recommended

O. basilicum is one of the most popular culinary herbs. There are dozens of varieties, including ones with large or tiny, green or purple and smooth or ruffled leaves.

Basil is a good companion plant for tomatoes—both like warm, moist growing conditions and when you pick tomatoes for a salad you'll also remember to include a few sprigs or leaves of basil.

Features: fragrant, decorative leaves
Height: 30–60 cm (12–24") **Spread:** 30–45 cm (12–18") **Hardiness:** tender annual

Borage
Borago

Borage is a vigorous, tenacious annual herb. It is valued by some but disliked by others because of its natural inclination to reseed itself everywhere. The flowers and foliage are not only pretty but also useful in salads and desserts.

Growing
Borage prefers **full sun. Moist, sandy, well-drained** soil is best. Borage is drought tolerant once established. Remove any unwanted seedlings as they emerge in early spring to prevent an onslaught of plants.

Tips
Plant borage in your vegetable or herb garden to attract bees for pollination. As an ornamental, it contrasts beautifully with dark foliage specimens.

Recommended
B. officinalis is an upright plant with high clusters of pendent, violet blue flowers in spring. The stems and foliage are covered in silvery hairs that complement the bluish flowers.

Young borage leaves are yummy in cool, raw salads, cold summer drinks or cooked with veggies. The flowers can be candied for decorating desserts.

Features: flowers, habit, fuzzy foliage and stems **Flower colour:** violet blue **Height:** 60–100 cm (24–36") **Spread:** 60 cm (24") **Hardiness:** zones 5–10

Chives
Allium

The delicate onion flavour of chives is best enjoyed fresh. Mix chives into dips or sprinkle them on salads and baked potatoes.

Growing

Chives grow best in **full sun**. The soil should be **fertile, moist** and **well drained**, but chives adapt to most soil conditions. These plants are easy to start from seed, but they do like the soil temperature to stay above 19° C (66° F) before they will germinate, so seeds started directly in the garden are unlikely to sprout before early summer.

Tips

Chives are decorative enough to be included in a mixed or herbaceous border and can be left to naturalize. In an herb garden, chives should be given plenty of space to allow self-seeding.

Recommended

A. schoenoprasum forms a clump of bright green cylindrical leaves. Clusters of pinky purple flowers are produced in early and mid-summer. Varieties with white or pink flowers are available.

Chives are said to increase appetite and encourage good digestion.

Features: foliage, form, flowers **Height:** 20–60 cm (8–24") **Spread:** 30 cm (12") or more **Hardiness:** zones 3–8

Coriander • Cilantro

Coriandrum

Coriander is a multi-purpose herb. The leaves, called cilantro, are used in salads, salsas and soups. The seeds, called coriander, are used in pies, chutneys and marmalades. Both have distinct flavours and culinary uses.

Growing

Coriander prefers **full sun** but tolerates partial shade. The soil should be **fertile, light** and **well drained**. These plants dislike humid conditions and do best during a dry summer.

Tips

Coriander has pungent leaves and is best planted where people will not have to brush past it. It is, however, a delight to behold when in flower. Add a plant or two here and there throughout your borders and vegetable garden, both for the visual appeal and to attract beneficial insects.

Recommended

C. sativum forms a clump of lacy basal foliage above which large, loose clusters of tiny, white flowers are produced. The seeds ripen in late summer and fall.

The delicate, cloud-like clusters of flowers attract pollinating insects such as butterflies and bees as well as abundant predatory insects that will help keep pest insects at a minimum in your garden.

Features: form, foliage, flowers, seeds
Height: 40–60 cm (16–24") **Spread:** 20–40 cm (8–16") **Hardiness:** tender annual

Dill

Anethum

Dill leaves and seeds are best known for their use as pickling herbs, though they have a wide variety of other culinary uses.

Growing

Dill grows best in **full sun** in a **sheltered** location out of strong winds. The soil should be of **poor to average fertility, moist** and **well drained**. Sow seeds every couple of weeks in spring and early summer to ensure a regular supply of leaves. Plants should not be grown near fennel because they will cross-pollinate and the seeds will lose their distinct flavours.

Tips

With its feathery leaves, dill is an attractive addition to a mixed bed or border. It can be included in a vegetable garden, but does well in any sunny location. It also attracts predatory insects to the garden.

Recommended

A. graveolens forms a clump of feathery foliage. Clusters of yellow flowers are borne at the tops of sturdy stems.

Dill turns up frequently in historical records as both a culinary and a medicinal herb. It was used by the Egyptians and Romans, and is mentioned in the Bible.

Features: feathery, edible foliage; yellow summer flowers; edible seeds **Height:** 60 cm–1.5 m (24"–5') **Spread:** 30 cm (12") or more **Hardiness:** annual

Lavender
Lavandula

All parts of the lavender plant are aromatic. The aroma is intensified when the foliage or flowers are touched, whether fresh or dried. The scent will evoke memories of warm summer days even in the depths of winter.

Growing

Lavenders grow best in **full sun**. The soil should be **average to fertile, alkaline** and **well drained**. In colder areas, lavenders should be covered with mulch and a good layer of snow. The key to winter survival is good drainage—often, winterkill results from wet 'feet,' not from cold.

Tips

Lavenders are wonderful edging plants. Good companions for these deer-resistant plants include other drought-tolerant specimens such as pinks, thyme, lamb's ears and sedum.

Recommended

L. angustifolia is an aromatic, bushy, tender perennial. From mid-summer to fall, it bears spikes of small flowers in varied shades of violet blue that stand above fragrant, silvery green foliage.

Also called: English lavender **Features:** fragrant flower spikes, silvery foliage **Flower colour:** purple, pink, blue **Height:** 20–60 cm (8–24") **Spread:** 30–60 cm (12–24") **Hardiness:** zones 4–8

Mint
Mentha

The cool, refreshing flavour of mint lends itself to tea and other hot or cold beverages. Mint sauce, made from freshly chopped leaves, is often served with lamb.

Growing
Mint grows well in **full sun** and **partial shade**. The soil should be **average to fertile, humus rich** and **moist**. These plants spread vigorously by rhizomes and will need a barrier in the soil to restrict their spread.

Tips
Mint is a good groundcover for damp spots. It grows well along ditches that may only be periodically wet. It also can be used in beds and borders, but may overwhelm less vigorous plants.

The flowers attract bees, butterflies and other pollinators to the garden.

Recommended
There are many species, hybrids and cultivars of mint. *M.* x *piperita* (peppermint), *M.* x *piperita citrata* (orange mint) and *M. spicata* (spearmint) are three of the most commonly grown culinary varieties. There are also more decorative varieties with variegated or curly leaves as well as varieties with unusual, fruit-scented leaves.

A few sprigs of fresh mint in a pitcher of iced tea gives it an added zip.

Features: fragrant foliage; purple, pink or white summer flowers **Height:** 15–90 cm (6–36") **Spread:** 90 cm (36") or more **Hardiness:** zones 3–8

Oregano • Marjoram
Origanum

Oregano and marjoram are two of the best-known and most frequently used herbs. They are popular in stuffings, soups and stews, and no pizza is complete until it has been sprinkled with fresh or dried oregano leaves.

Growing

Oregano and marjoram grow best in **full sun**. The soil should be of **poor to average fertility, neutral to alkaline** and **well drained**. The flowers attract pollinators to the garden.

Tips

These bushy perennials make a lovely addition to any border and can be trimmed to form low hedges.

Recommended

O. majorana (marjoram) is upright and shrubby with light green, hairy leaves. It bears white or pink flowers in summer and can be grown as an annual where it is not hardy.

O. vulgare hirtum (oregano, Greek oregano) is the most flavourful culinary variety of oregano. The low, bushy plant has hairy, grey-green leaves and bears white flowers. Many other interesting varieties of *O. vulgare* are available, including those with golden, variegated or curly leaves.

In Greek oros means 'mountain' and ganos means 'joy and beauty,' so oregano translates as 'joy or beauty of the mountain.'

Features: fragrant foliage, white or pink summer flowers, bushy habit **Height:** 30–80 cm (12–32") **Spread:** 20–45 cm (8–18") **Hardiness:** zones 4–8

Parsley
Petroselinum

Though usually used as a garnish, parsley is rich in vitamins and minerals and is reputed to freshen the breath after garlic or onion-rich foods are eaten.

Growing
Parsley grows well in **full sun** or **partial shade**. The soil should be of **average to rich fertility, humus rich, moist** and **well drained**. Direct sow seeds; this plant resents transplanting. If you start seeds early, use peat pots so the plants can be potted or planted out without disruption.

Tips
Parsley should be started where you mean to grow it. Containers of parsley can be kept close to the house for easy picking.

The bright green leaves and compact growth habit make parsley a good edging plant for beds and borders.

Recommended
P. crispum forms a clump of bright green, divided leaves. This plant is biennial, but is usually grown as an annual. Cultivars may have flat or curly leaves. Flat leaves are more flavourful and curly are more decorative. Dwarf cultivars are available.

Features: attractive foliage **Height:** 20–60 cm (8–24") **Spread:** 30–60 cm (12–24") **Hardiness:** tender annual

Rosemary
Rosmarinus

The needle-like leaves of rosemary are used to flavour a wide variety of culinary dishes, including chicken, pork, lamb, rice, tomato and egg dishes.

Growing

Rosemary prefers **full sun**, but tolerates partial shade. The soil should be of **poor to average fertility** and **well drained**.

Tips

Rosemary grows best in a container as a specimen or in a mixed border or bed. Low-growing, spreading plants can be included in a rock garden or grown in hanging baskets. Upright forms can be trained as topiary specimens.

Recommended

R. officinalis is a dense, bushy evergreen shrub with narrow, dark green leaves. The habit varies somewhat between cultivars from strongly upright to prostrate and spreading. Flowers are usually in shades of blue, but pink-flowered cultivars are available. Cultivars are available that can survive in zone 6 in a sheltered location with winter protection. Plants rarely reach their mature size when grown in containers.

To overwinter a container-grown plant, keep it in very light or partial shade in summer, then put it in a sunny window indoors for winter and keep it well watered, but not soaking wet.

Features: fragrant, evergreen foliage; bright blue, sometimes pink, summer flowers **Height:** 20 cm–1.2 m (8"–4')
Spread: 30 cm–1.2 m (12"–4')
Hardiness: tender annual

Sage
Salvia

Sage is perhaps best known as a flavouring for stuffing, but it has a great range of uses, including in soups, stews, sausages and dumplings.

Growing

Sage prefers **full sun** but tolerates light shade. The soil should be of **average fertility** and **well drained**. These plants benefit from a light mulch of compost each year. They are drought tolerant once established.

Tips

Sage is an attractive plant for the border. It adds volume to the middle of the border and makes an attractive edging or feature plant near the front. Sage can also be grown in mixed planters.

Recommended

S. officinalis is a woody, mounding plant with soft, grey-green leaves. Spikes of light purple flowers appear in early and mid-summer. Many cultivars with attractive foliage are available, including the silver-leaved 'Berggarten,' the yellow-margined 'Icterina,' the purple-leaved 'Purpurea,' and the purple-green and cream variegated 'Tricolor,' which has a pink flush to the new growth.

Sage has been used since at least ancient Greek times as a medicinal and culinary herb. It continues to be widely used for both those purposes today.

Features: fragrant decorative foliage, blue or purple summer flowers
Height: 30–60 cm (12–24")
Spread: 45–90 cm (18–36")
Hardiness: zones 4–8

Thyme

Thymus

These plants are bee magnets when blooming; thyme honey is pleasantly herbal and goes very well with biscuits.

Thyme is a popular culinary herb used in soups, stews, casseroles and with roasts.

Growing

Thyme prefers **full sun**. The soil should be **neutral to alkaline** and of **poor to average fertility. Good drainage** is essential. It is beneficial to work leaf mould and sharp limestone gravel into the soil to improve structure and drainage.

Tips

Thyme is useful for sunny, dry locations at the front of borders, between or beside paving stones, on rock gardens and rock walls, and in containers.

Once the plants have finished flowering, shear them back by about half to encourage new growth and prevent the plants from becoming too woody.

Recommended

T. x *citriodorus* (lemon-scented thyme) forms a mound of lemon-scented, dark green foliage. The flowers are pale pink. Cultivars with silver- or gold-margined leaves are available.

T. pseudolanuginosus (woolly thyme) forms a fuzzy grey-green mat of foliage covered in light pink flowers. It is one of the hardiest groundcovers available.

Features: bushy habit; fragrant, decorative foliage; purple, pink or white flowers **Height:** 20–40 cm (8–16") **Spread:** 20–40 cm (8–16") **Hardiness:** zones 2–8

Castor Bean

Ricinus

This vigorous annual can reach enormous sizes in relatively short time. Its exotic leaves and large stature are ideally suited to large informal beds, and it makes a great impact in containers.

Growing

Castor bean requires a location in **full sun**. The soil should be **rich** and **loose** with **good drainage**. It requires little care and is very tolerant to hot and dry conditions.

Tips

Castor bean suits background plantings and borders because it grows so quickly. It can totally obscure unsightly areas, including garbage cans, air conditioners, utility boxes and meters, in a short period of time. Though this plant grows well in containers, a small container may stunt its overall growth.

Contact with castor bean's nicked or damaged seeds, spiny seedpods and leaves may cause an allergic reaction. **All parts are considered to be poisonous—do not eat!**

Recommended

R. communis produces huge, deeply lobed, palm-like leaves. Spiky, rounded seedpods follow after the unimpressive colourful flower clusters are spent.

Features: large, ornate foliage; growth habit
Height: 2.5–3 m (8–10') **Spread:** 1.5–2 m
(5–7') **Hardiness:** tender annual, not frost hardy

Clover
Trifolium

I came across this plant by accident one summer and found it ideal for many different uses. It looked stunning all summer long, planted alongside 'Gartenmeister Bonstedt' fuschia and 'Peekaboo' spilanthes.

Growing
Black-leaved clover is best grown in **full to part sun**. The soil should be **moist** but **well drained** and with a **neutral pH**.

Tips
This lovely little plant will add interest to containers or the edge of mixed borders. It's especially striking when planted next to other dramatically coloured foliage and bright, contrasting flowers. It also works well in trough and rock gardens.

Recommended
Choose from a variety of clover species and cultivars. Foliage comes in green, maroon, chocolate brown or a combination of the three. Its pompom flowers can be pink, red, yellow and white, and a recent cultivar offers an even more dramatic look. *T. repens* **'Purpurascens Quadrifolium'** (black-leaved clover), a fast-growing tender perennial, produces typical clover leaves with dark burgundy centres surrounded by bright green. It may produce small, pea-like, white flowers in late summer.

The Trifolium genus encompasses all clovers. Trifolium plants have spreading growth habits, and each stem can produce three to five leaflets. Retailers often refer to Trifolium specimens as 'clover-like' or lump them into the Oxalis group so as not to scare away gardeners who fear clover.

Also called: Dutch clover, shamrock, white clover **Features:** colourful foliage, growth habit, pom-pom flowers **Height:** 8–30 cm (3–10") **Spread:** 30–45 cm (10–18") **Hardiness:** zones 4–8

Fescue

Festuca

Fescue grass was one of the first ornamental grasses to appear on the market over a decade ago and is now relatively common throughout the prairies. Fescue thrives in harsh conditions and continues to display its finest features.

Growing

Fescue prefers a **full sun** location in **poor to moderately fertile** soil that is **well drained** and a little on the **dry** side.

Tips

Fescue is valued for its low-growing tufts of foliage. It is frequently used in xeriscape settings, contemporary gardens and naturalized areas. Low-growing fescue also works well in rock and alpine gardens.

Recommended

F. glauca produces steely blue tufts of fine, needle-like blades of grass. Most varieties produce tan-coloured spikes that emerge from mounds of blue grass, revealing small, tan flower plumes. A great many cultivars and hybrids are available.

Fescue specimens can be divided and replanted approximately every two to three years or when they begin to die out in the centres. This will help to maintain their foliar colour.

Features: foliar colour and form, flower spikes, growth habit **Height:** 15–45 cm (6–18")
Spread: 25–30 cm (10–12")
Hardiness: zones 3–8

Flowering Fern
Osmunda

The fern is an ancient plant with a pre-historic mystique. It isn't hard to imagine primitive reptiles and massive amphibians resting under the fern fronds millions of years ago.

Growing

Flowering ferns prefer **light shade**, but tolerate full sun if the soil is consistently moist. Soil should be **fertile**, **humus rich**, **acidic** and **moist**. This fern will tolerate wet soil.

The 'flowers' of flowering ferns are not actually flowers at all. They are the spore-producing sporangia.

Tips

These large ferns form an attractive mass when planted in large colonies. Include them in beds and borders or in a woodland garden.

Recommended

O. cinnamomea (cinnamon fern) has light green fronds that fan out in a circular fashion from a central point. Leafless, cinnamon brown, fertile fronds are produced in spring and stand straight up in the center of the plant. It grows 75 cm–1.5 m (30"–5') tall and spreads 60–90 cm (24–36") wide. (Zones 2–8)

O. regalis (royal fern) forms a dense clump of foliage. Feathery, flower-like, fertile fronds stand out amongst the sterile fronds in summer and mature to a rusty brown. It grows 90 cm–2 m (3–7') tall and spreads 90 cm–4 m (3–13') wide. (Zones 3–8)

Features: perennial fern, decorative fertile fronds, habit **Height:** 75 cm–2 m (30"–7')
Spread: 60 cm–4 m (2–13')
Hardiness: zones 2–8

Maidenhair Fern

Adiantum

These charming and delicate-looking ferns add grace to any woodland planting. For a touch of whimsy, tuck a garden gnome or other small ornament beneath the fronds to peer out at passersby.

Growing

Maidenhair fern grows well in **light** or **partial shade** and tolerates full shade. Soil should be of **average fertility, humus rich** and **moist**. This fern rarely needs dividing, but can be divided in spring to propagate more plants.

Tips

These lovely ferns grace any shaded spot in the garden. Include them in rock gardens, woodland gardens and shaded borders, or beneath shade trees where the grass grows thin if it grows at all. They also look attractive next to a shaded water feature.

Recommended

A. pedatum forms a spreading mound of delicate arching fronds. Light green leaflets stand out against black stems, and the whole plant turns bright yellow in fall.

There are many more species of maidenhair fern, but most are grown in greenhouses or as houseplants because they are not hardy to Canadian conditions.

Also called: northern maidenhair
Features: perennial fern, summer and fall foliage, habit **Height:** 30–60 cm (12–24")
Spread: 30–60 cm (12–24")
Hardiness: zones 2–8

Miscanthus
Miscanthus

One of the most widely grown ornamental grasses available, Miscanthus offers vivid colours and ornamental plumes, and needs little maintenance. Most of the varied species and cultivars are hardy to the harsh prairie environment.

Growing

Miscanthus tolerates most conditions but prefers locations in **full sun**. Moderately **moist, fertile** but **well-drained** soil is best.

The fan-shaped plumes are ideal for cutting, for use in crafts, and for fresh and dried arrangements.

Tips

Miscanthus is most effective when planted en masse in a naturalized area or mixed border. Some of the varieties available can grow to be quite large and may be best displayed as specimens. If left alone in fall and winter, the dried foliage and showy plumes look beautiful in the snow.

Recommended

A great many species, cultivars and hybrids that offer varied foliar colour and tall, ornate plumes are available. The majority are variegated, striped or speckled with one or more colours, and most produce showy, persistent plumes. Find out what is available at your local garden centre.

Features: colourful, decorative, strap-like foliage and showy plumes; winter interest
Height: 90 cm–2.4 m (3–8') **Spread:** 60 cm–1.2 m (24"–4') **Hardiness:** zones 3–8

Ostrich Fern
Matteuccia

These ferns are prized for their delicious, emerging spring fronds as well as for their ornamental foliage and habit.

Growing
Ostrich fern prefers **partial** or **light shade**, but tolerates full shade. Soil should be **average to fertile, humus rich, neutral to acidic** and **moist**.

Tips
This fern appreciates a moist woodland garden and is often found growing wild along the edges of woodland streams and creeks. Useful in shaded borders, these plants are quick to spread, to the delight of those who have tasted the delicate young fronds.

Recommended
M. struthiopteris (*M. pennsylvanica*) forms a circular cluster of slightly arching fronds. Stiff, brown, fertile fronds poke up in the center of the cluster in late summer and persist through the winter.

The tightly coiled, new spring fronds taste delicious lightly steamed and served with butter. Remove the bitter, papery, reddish brown coating before steaming.

Also called: fiddlehead fern **Features:** perennial fern, foliage, habit **Height:** 90 cm–1.5 m (3–5')
Spread: 30–90 cm (12–36") or more
Hardiness: zones 1–8

Reed Grass

Calamagrostis

Reed grass is highly sought after and frequently used by landscape designers who appreciate its upright, architectural appearance.

Growing

Reed grass thrives in **full to partial sun**. The soil should be **moist, humus rich** and **well drained**. It is tolerant of even the poorest soils.

Tips

Reed grass is ideal for mixed borders and xeriscaped spaces. The long, elegant inflorescences add beauty to a winter landscape and last well into spring.

Cutting all stems down to the crown or to the ground in early spring will allow for new growth as the days become warmer.

Recommended

C. x *acutiflora* is a slow-growing perennial grass that grows into a clump of arching, narrow, green blades of grass. Tall, wiry stems emerge from the clump, bearing silvery bronze to pale purple-brown panicles of flowers. Decorative cultivars are available in varied sizes and colours.

Also called: smallweed, feather reed grass
Features: decorative flower stems, foliage, habit **Height:** 60 cm–1.5 m (24"–5') **Spread:** 60 cm–1.2 m (24"–4') **Hardiness:** zones 3–8

Rush

Juncus

Rush is a foliar specimen but it's often mistaken for a grass. The stems are hollow and cylindrical rather than flat and broad like leaves. This unique plant is a must for any type of water-related garden.

Growing

Rush prefers **sun** or **partial shade**. The soil should be **consistently moist, if not wet**, and **slightly acidic**. It can be grown in a small container or submerged in water to its crown in a water feature or pond.

Tips

Rush is considered a marginal perennial. It is well suited to bog gardens, locations that remain moist for long periods and water gardens.

Recommended

J. effusus (rush) is a tender perennial wetland plant that grows in a clump and spreads by vigorous underground rhizomes. Erect clumps of slightly arching cylindrical stems can grow up to 90 cm (36"). **'Cuckoo'** has longitudinal yellow stripes, while **'Spiralis'** (corkscrew rush) is a low-growing rush with curly, spiraling stems. **'Unicorn'** is an exaggerated version of 'Spiralis,' producing thicker, longer, curled stems. **'Vittatus'** has narrow, creamy white bands and 'Zebrinus' has broad white bands.

Rush can overwinter outdoors if buried in a well-protected, moist area and covered with several inches of bark mulch or leaf matter. It can also be brought indoors and treated as a houseplant until its return outdoors in the spring.

Features: foliage, form, versatility **Height:** 45–90 cm (18–36") **Spread:** 30–90 cm (12–36") **Hardiness:** zones 4–8

Sensitive Fern

Onoclea

Sensitive yes, but only to frost. Otherwise, this little fern is quite tough. The common name came from early settlers, who observed the fronds' sensitivity to frost.

Growing

Sensitive fern grows best in **light shade** but tolerates full shade and partial shade. The fronds can scorch if exposed to too m uch sun. Soil should be **fertile, humus rich, slightly acidic** and **moist**. A sheltered location with protection from the wind is best.

Tips

Sensitive ferns like to live in damp, shady places. Include them in shaded borders, woodland gardens and other sheltered locations.

Recommended

O. sensibilis forms a mass of light green, arching fronds. Plants grow about 60 cm (24") tall and can spread indefinitely. Fertile fronds are produced in late summer and persist through the winter.

Sensitive fern is native to the woodlands and shaded streambanks of eastern North America.

Features: deciduous perennial fern, attractive foliage, habit **Height:** 60 cm (24")
Spread: indefinite **Hardiness:** zones 3–8

Sweet Woodruff

Galium

Sweet woodruff is a groundcover that abounds with good qualities, including attractive light green foliage that smells like new-mown hay, abundant white spring flowers and the ability to fill in garden spaces without taking over.

Growing

This plant prefers **partial shade**. It will grow well, but will not bloom well, in full shade. Soil should be **humus rich** and **evenly moist**.

Tips

Sweet woodruff is a perfect woodland groundcover. It forms a beautiful green carpet and thrives in the same conditions as azaleas and rhododendrons. Shear it back after it blooms to encourage growth of foliage that will crowd out weeds.

Recommended

G. odoratum is a low, spreading groundcover. Clusters of star-shaped, white flowers appear in a flush in late spring and occur sporadically through mid-summer.

The dried leaves of sweet woodruff were once used to scent bed linens and freshen stale rooms.

Features: perennial groundcover; white, late-spring to mid-summer flowers; fragrant foliage; habit **Height:** 30–45 cm (12–18")
Spread: indefinite **Hardiness:** zones 3–8

Switch Grass

Panicum

Growing

Switch grass prefers locations in **full sun**. This ornamental grass tolerates a wide range of soil conditions but thrives in **fertile, well-drained** conditions.

Tips

Switch grass offers multi-season interest, so choosing a location for it isn't usually difficult. It's best planted within a mixed border where its best attributes can be displayed throughout fall and winter.

Recommended

P. virgatum produces airy flowers atop tall, wiry stems that emerge through narrow, arching blades of grass. A variety of cultivars offer different foliar colours, including metallic blue and green, throughout the summer. The fall colours are particularly stunning.

Don't panic if you find this genus growing in your garden. Its other common name, panic grass, was derived from panicum, *the Latin word for millet.*

Also called: panic grass **Features:** colourful foliage and flowery plumes, distinctive growth habit **Height:** 90 cm–15 m (3–5') **Spread:** 90 cm–1.2 m (3–4') **Hardiness:** zones 3–8

Glossary

Acid soil: soil with a pH lower than 7.0

Annual: a plant that germinates, flowers, sets seed and dies in one growing season

Alkaline soil: soil with a pH higher than 7.0

Basal leaves: leaves that form from the crown, at the base of the plant

Bract: a modified leaf at the base of a flower or flower cluster

Corm: a bulblike, food-storing, underground stem, resembling a bulb without scales

Crown: the part of the plant at or just below soil level where the shoots join the roots

Cultivar: a cultivated plant variety with one or more distinct differences from the species, e.g., in flower colour or disease resistance

Damping off: fungal disease causing seedlings to rot at soil level and topple over

Deadhead: to remove spent flowers to maintain a neat appearance and encourage a longer blooming season

Direct sow: to sow seeds directly in the garden

Dormancy: a period of plant inactivity, usually during winter or unfavourable conditions

Double flower: a flower with an unusually large number of petals

Genus: a category of biological classification between the species and family levels; the first word in a scientific name indicates the genus

Grafting: a type of propagation in which a stem or bud of one plant is joined onto the rootstock of another plant of a closely related species

Hardy: capable of surviving unfavourable conditions, such as cold weather or frost, without protection

Hip: the fruit of a rose, containing the seeds

Humus: decomposed or decomposing organic material in the soil

Hybrid: a plant resulting from natural or human-induced cross-breeding between varieties, species or genera

Inflorescence: a flower cluster

Neutral soil: soil with a pH of 7.0

Perennial: a plant that takes three or more years to complete its life cycle

pH: a measure of acidity or alkalinity; the soil pH influences availability of nutrients for plants

Rhizome: a root-like, food-storing stem that grows horizontally at or just below soil level, from which new shoots may emerge

Rootball: the root mass and surrounding soil of a plant

Seedhead: dried, inedible fruit that contains seeds; the fruiting stage of the inflorescence

Self-seeding: reproducing by means of seeds without human assistance, so that new plants constantly replace those that die

Semi-double flower: a flower with petals in two or three rings

Single flower: a flower with a single ring of typically four or five petals

Species: the fundamental unit of biological classification; the entity from which cultivars and varieties are derived

Standard: a shrub or small tree grown with an erect main stem, accomplished either through pruning and training or by grafting the plant onto a tall, straight stock

Sucker: a shoot that comes up from the root, often some distance from the plant; it can be separated to form a new plant once it develops its own roots

Tender: incapable of surviving the climatic conditions of a given region and requiring protection from frost or cold

Tuber: the thick section of a rhizome bearing nodes and buds

Variegation: foliage that has more than one colour, often patched or striped or bearing leaf margins of a different colour

Variety: a naturally occurring variant of a species

Index